AT

a book about the sea

SWIM

Brendan Mac Evilly has written for *The Irish Times*, *The Sunday Times*, *The Stinging Fly*, *Cara* and *We Are Dublin*. He has worked with the Irish Writers' Centre, Publishing Ireland and a number of publishing houses in Dublin and Oxford. He loves lounging in the sea for five minutes, then burning the ear off his fellow swimmers for the next hour.

Michael O'Reilly is an actor and writer who has performed on stage and the big screen in Ireland and abroad. His favourite way of entering the water is fast and furious.

Brendan Mac Evilly (left) and Michael O'Reilly (right) at the Forty Foot, Dublin.
Background and previous page: The crashing waves at Coumeenoole, County Kerry.

CAUTION

Like any water-based activity, wild swimming has risks and can be dangerous. The author and The Collins Press accept no responsibility for any injury, loss or inconvenience sustained by anyone reading this book. Swimming, jumping, diving or any other activities at any of these locations is entirely at your own risk.

AT

a book about the sea

SWIM

Brendan Mac Evilly

with Michael O'Reilly

The Collins Press

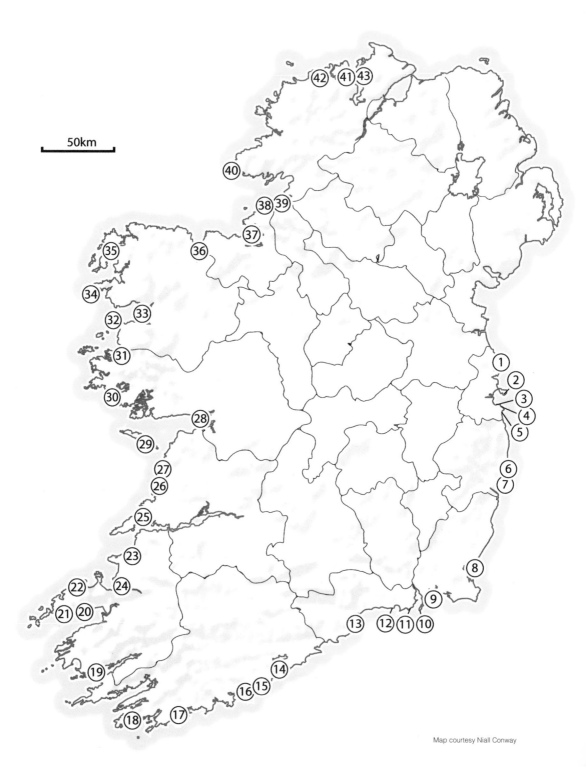

50km

Map courtesy Niall Conway

CONTENTS

ACKNOWLEDGEMENTS

For those who embark on making a book, it is usually a lonely journey. However, the creation of this title relied directly on a great number of people. It was Michael O'Reilly who convinced me that it couldn't be done alone and that he was the right person to join me. An actor and comedian, Michael is a natural charmer. As a writer, he has a keen sense of narrative, which has shaped our journey. He has a sharp photographic eye and strong organising instinct. It would have been a very different journey, and book, without him. We would like to offer our sincerest thanks to all our Kickstarter backers – family, friends and strangers – without whom we simply wouldn't have been able to publish the first edition of the book; to the swimmers and the swimming clubs we swam with along the way: the Wexford Masters, the swimmers at Helvick Cove, the Myrtleville swimmers, GTown Surf School, the Sandycove swimmers, Steve Black, Wild Water Adventures, and the North West Surf School; to those who went above and beyond in helping us on our journey: the Mahon Family, Jolly and Henry Ronan, Patricia Fitzpatrick, Johnny St John, Eileen and Francis Ryan, Jackie Roantree, the Gannon family, Niamh McGrath and Damian Schwarz, Eva Reilly, Sinead Gaughan, Liz Healy, the Broadhaven Bay Hotel, the Talbot Hotel, the Keane Family, and Terry Tedstone; to the writers, photographers and artists who feature in the book, for sharing your words, images and passion for the sea; to the hundreds of people who suggested these fantastic swimming spots; to Lisa Timmermann for her photography on the east coast; to Matthew Parkinson-Bennett for a fantastic job editing the text; to Conor Purcell for helping us to bring our idea to fruition; to Emer Mullane for her excellent media management and PR work; to all at The Collins Press; to Hannah for her love and belief in the project, and her editorial expertise; to our dads, Niall Mac Evilly and Michael O'Reilly, for taking us to the sea.

PHOTOGRAPH CREDITS

Pádraig Burke: pp. 72, 73, 85

Molly Keane: pp. 177, 178

Aoife Mac Evilly: p. 103

Emer Mullane: pp. 22, 23, 25

Siobhan Russell: pp. 68, 70

Terry Tedstone: pp. 186, 188

Peter Wallace: pp. 117

Patricia Fitzpatrick: pp. 116

Hannah Lloyd: pp. 12, 13, 16, 151

Rosemarie Mangan: p. 154

Eberhard Rapp: pp. 187, 188

Peter Sellers: pp. 84, 87

Lisa Timmermann: pp. 2, 10, 28, 29, 48, 49, 52, 60, 61, 62

All other photographs © Michael O'Reilly and Brendan Mac Evilly

FOREWORD

Water and emotions, both run deep. For swimmers, the connections to particular places play out across their lives and deepen in their bodies and hearts, in the same way that an underwater piece of metal becomes encrusted with the layers of algae, seaweed, rust and shells that mark out its natural resilience. At the same time, there is a deep joy that builds up for most swimmers across their lifetime of swimming, even when they no longer swim. These twin elements – joy and connection – are central to the wellness in people's lives and are beautifully illustrated in this wild, free-flowing book. Brendan and Michael take us on a journey that, quite frankly, most of us are extremely jealous of. Who wouldn't want to take off for a summer jaunt along the coast, jumping in and out of waters, lives, pubs and homes, while at the same time spending quality time with old mates, new acquaintances and the eternal kindnesses of strangers? This book explores swimming spots in eleven of the island of Ireland's seventeen coastal counties and visits beaches, coves, tidal pools, baths, sea loughs and islands. Each is different yet the same, and reflects the love and care of the people who inhabit it. The character of the place emerges naturally from the characters in the place and Brendan and Michael's stories are told in a modest yet careful way to emphasise this fact. Every swimming spot has its history and stories. Some are truthful, some are, as an oral historian once said, 'in the parish of truth'. Many are absolute whoppers, usually ones associated with characters like Richard Harris or his old mucker in Kilkee, Manuel Di Lucia. As a child in the 1960s and 1970s I used to go to Kilkee and hear those same stories and can confirm that they were as believable then as they are now. Many of the more remote swimming spots used to be for men only, in part due to the tendency of men to swim naked and frighten children and horses in Victorian times, for which they were banished to remote and often dangerous spots around the coast. Yet many of the most ardent and hardiest swimmers now are women and a reclaiming of the coast makes it a place for all. While I have also heard it argued that swimming is very much a middle-class thing, the stories in this book are ageless, classless and priceless. They span everything from the first frightening yet thrilling leap into the unknown blue, to the ninety-year-olds who have repeated their daily dip for years. There is a natural promiscuity to the act – our authors swim with anyone, anytime, anywhere. Yet what is most striking about the book is the way that Brendan and Michael use very modern means – various forms of social media – to charm their way into a series of ever-welcoming communities. These swimming communities (though we shouldn't forget the lone swimmer) are the real custodians of swimming places in Ireland and I see this book as reflecting that communal power, to build, restore, maintain and create new places for people to gather and share. As a swimmer at the Guillamene once said when asked if he was scared of drowning at sea, 'sure you'd only be swapping one paradise for another'. *At Swim* gives us a glimpse of a paradise that we can all enjoy, so – enjoy.

RONAN FOLEY
Maynooth University Department of Geography

Kids leap from the small pier on the western side of the beach at Derrynane, County Kerry.

Introduction

t's difficult to avoid religious analogies when speaking about sea swimming. For some people it's a daily rite. More moderate followers might go once a week. Others again only on special occasions – perhaps on Christmas Day after being forced by a more militant family member. But all who take the plunge are believers to some degree. The experience is almost spiritual. There is a literal cleansing. It is often a communal ritual, where you shed your clothes in the company of others, and enter the temple. There is, at the same time, an isolation – in the sea you are disconnected from the temporal world and its difficulties. The distraction that the bracing water provides, and the need to focus on the simple process of keeping afloat, swimming, help to clear the mind. For a few minutes you are freed from the constant flow of your thoughts. The sea is a source of healing too. People have been 'taking the waters' for centuries. Swimmers claim the sea relieves aches and ills of all kinds, from hangovers to sciatica, from diabetes to depression. More importantly, swimming in the sea is incredible fun. It generates a natural high.

Brendan swims up the gully into Solomon's Hole, The Hook, County Wexford.

In the dark days of a winter as Ireland eased out of the depths of recession, I was managing to swim in the sea only about once a month. After an unusually hot summer full of weekly dips, I was becoming what you might call a lapsed swimmer. I dreamed of summer days, with longer swims in warmer waters. I had bathed in many of Dublin's famous spots but knew only vaguely of others around the Irish coastline. Wherever I swam, there was always a kind word from a stranger – a willingness to talk that is more commonly shied away from. I imagined a journey to places further afield, hearing the stories of innumerable strangers, listening to the local lore connected with each spot, and sampling the cool seawater daily. It was in those dark days that Michael O'Reilly and I decided to spend the coming summer months tracing Ireland's coastline in search of enticing entries to the sea. The purpose of this book is not to provide a definitive list of the best places to swim, but rather to give an impression of Ireland's sea-swimming culture at a moment in time and give voice to the stories attached to the places where we enter the sea.

We hope this book brings more swimmers to the sea, with a greater respect for the guardians who develop and maintain these locations, a greater sense of the sea-bathing culture that surrounds them, and a greater appreciation for the power of the sea and the joy it can bring.

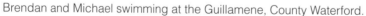

Brendan and Michael swimming at the Guillamene, County Waterford.

Dublin

1

Barnacled granite typical of the Dublin coastline.

1 Skerries

'I remember writing something as a young lad, maybe I was about sixteen,' says Kevin Curran, remembering his early efforts at prose. 'There's a scene in it where we're up to our waists in water, looking back on the coast.' Kevin can't quite remember if it actually happened or if a merger of faction and fiction has taken place. 'I remember writing the scene,' he says, 'but it feels like a memory.' Twenty years on, Kevin is a published novelist as well as teacher in his hometown of Balbriggan, but he still swims daily between May and October to draw from the well of inspiration.

It's early July and I'm out at the tip of Skerries where Kevin is showing me Red Island's two swimming spots: the Captains and the Springers. There doesn't seem to be much between them in either distance (about 200m) or appearance (both are concrete shelves laid on natural rock with steps into the sea). But, being a creature of habit, like many a swimmer, Kevin has only ever swum at the Springers, so that's where we go for our first dip.

For Kevin, the sea is more than just a place to swim. 'Being in the sea, you get a sense of openness. The ocean gives you space to think, to fill with your own thoughts. When you're in, on a beautiful day, you want to enjoy it. It gives you a sense of time and space – an unlimited horizon.'

And Kevin, like myself, is partial to an evening swim. 'There's something spiritual about it. You get that otherworldly feeling.' He tells me about a

Sunset at the Captains on Red Island.

Kevin Curran (right) and Brendan watching the sunset at the Captains.

third novel he plans to write, currently in the early development stages.

'Half of it is set on a fishing trawler. All that I know at this stage is a rough outline of the story, which I'm not going to tell you because I don't want to talk it out. But *At Sea* is the title.

'Coming from Balbriggan, I know a lot of people who are fishermen. I've taught a lot of fishermen's children who have since become fishermen themselves. I'm going to go out on my friend Greg's boat. He's been fishing fifteen years and his dad is a fisherman too. The book is about a father/son relationship, so I'm mad to talk to them.'

'Does Greg swim at all?' I ask. 'Greg came down for a swim with me about three weeks ago. He was in for two minutes and got out; he couldn't hack it.'

I wonder about the old tradition of fishermen purposely not learning to swim. 'There was a death here about four years ago,' says Kevin, 'just before we moved into our new home in Skerries. Two local fishermen were found about twenty miles north of here. It was a huge deal. I remember Greg saying, "That's why I don't wear a life jacket", because the victims both had

Brendan takes his camera for a swim to get this picture of Kevin.

life jackets on them when they were found. There was a great rallying of the community to raise funds to keep the search going for them.' As the summer wears on I wonder how Kevin is doing. Has he swum at the Captains yet? So in early September, when our journey of the coastline is nearly complete, I send Kevin a text to see if I can get him out for another swim. The forecast for the evening is for clear skies.

We head again to Red Island. 'The Captains is the one you want to swim at this time,' Kevin says. He has spent the summer swimming at his usual spot without exception, but is more than happy to make this evening's swim his first dip across the way. The full tide is an hour away, ideal for the Captains, which is home to the Frosties, a group of daily swimmers who have been swimming every morning for the past sixteen years, growing in numbers steadily. Kevin's aunt, Anne Laird, is a long-time member of the Frosties, and he has invited her to join us.

At high tide the Captains is flooded. If the tide is too high at 11 a.m., the Frosties come across to the Springers. Like other casual bathing clubs at the Forty Foot and Guillamene in Waterford, the late morning seems to be a good time to congregate for the social swimmer. Perhaps a lonely time of day, the Jeremy Kyle hour, which is best filled with an invigorating swim.

As the sun sets, the water is calm, cool and syrupy, and I risk taking 'the good camera' into the sea with me, kicking madly to keep afloat. Kevin reminds me that the North Beach leading out to Red Island (actually a peninsula) is the only beach in Dublin with a view of the sunset as it faces west, back in towards the mainland. The sun just about makes it around to shine on the Captains too, laying a pink light on the heads of the two seals bobbing beside us throughout our swim.

We dry off and make the short walk over to the Springers and find Kevin's aunt, Anne, and her friend Anne Carroll, another of the Frosties. They had come to meet us but presumed we'd be here at Kevin's usual spot. They're just out of the water themselves. Anne Laird speaks of her slow-building relationship with sea swimming. It was more than thirty years ago that she learned to swim, when she was in her thirties, but only in the last fifteen years did she take her first dip in the sea. The carrot of a Christmas swim drew her in one summer, in the belief that if she swam every day from then till December she'd be able to bear the cold of the midwinter plunge. She hasn't looked back.

Some of the Frosties are mere dippers like myself, in the water for ten minutes, then chatting away for the next half hour. But others in the group have been adding distance to their swims. Anne points out a route called 'the M50' which begins at either the Springers or the Captains, cuts clockwise to the South Beach, out of the water and 50m walk over the road, then sets off again from the North Beach, around the pier head at Skerries Harbour and back to your clothes, towel and flask of tea – a full circle of Red Island. The route is reversed depending on the flow of the tide. Others have been setting the nearby Colt and St Patrick's Islands in their sights with a small number having swum as far as Rockabill Island, 7km off the coast.

Anne Carroll is very knowledgeable about the sea. She says that September is a good month to swim as the sea is iodine rich. Iodine is released by the seaweed and absorbed through our skin, and is an essential mineral required by every cell in our bodies.

It's Anne's third swim of the day, despite having spotted five Lion's Mane jellyfish at the Captains earlier that morning, a rare sighting in Irish waters this summer. She's clearly someone who sees the value of a daily dip. As Kevin says, 'It doesn't do anyone any harm to step outside themselves. For ten or fifteen minutes of the day you leave everything behind in a little bundle on the steps. Your troubles never follow you. Especially not in Ireland where it's too cold to think of anything else.'

Kevin and Brendan getting changed at the Captains.

SKERRIES

Latitude: 53.583981
Longitude: -6.100279

Type: Two bathing areas, distance swims, bathing.

When: High to low tide, Springers only at higher tides.

Access: Through Skerries, onto Harbour Road, right at the end of the pier. Parking available.

Safety: Springers is more sheltered and therefore safer. Sign reads 'Competent Swimmers Only' at both spots.

2 Howth

Travelling from Dublin city, take a right at Sutton Cross, drive along the Carrickbrack Road for 3km, and take a right onto Ceanchor Road, which trails off into a dirt track leading to the cliff walk. This is usually the anticlimactic end of the cliff walk for those who begin their journey at Howth village – who have walked for hours only to realise they have another 3km walk through suburbia to the DART station. But if, on the other hand, you make this your starting point, and take a right turn once you hit the coastal path, a 300m walk will bring you to a relatively safe scrabble down the cliff face to a sandy cove, known as Drumleck Beach or Jameson's Pool.

I have been here twice before but it's still difficult to work out if we are at the right location; we wonder if we should walk along a little further. From a height you are looking for a diamond shape in water, cut out by a

View of Jameson's Pool from the cliff walk above.

cement wall laid by members of the Jameson family in the early part of the twentieth century. At high tide Michael and I find the walls of the pool entirely submerged. To kill time while the tide peels away, we double back on our route and head towards the lighthouse in search of the Lion's Head, aka the Baily Jumps – a small headland set about halfway between the beach and the lighthouse. On the cliff walk, we meet a group of lads in their early twenties. They are hanging over a fence, looking down the cliff with a mixture of fear and excitement. Of course, we can't know this for certain, but that's what we are feeling: Michael feeling excitement and me fear.

The Lion's Head has been in use as a swimming spot for over a hundred years. In the early 1900s a university professor and his students popularised it, building steps down the sheer cliff face and adding diving boards, changing shelters and a latrine. But now the steps have fallen away. A dusty dirt track is left in their place, the sea only accessible now with the use of a rope to abseil down. The diving boards are long gone, but the concrete steps to which the boards were fixed are still in situ. Instead of maintaining the steps and

Young lads diving from the Lion's Head.

Jameson's Pool. The pool is invisible when submerged at high tide.

boards, the council have preferred to fence them off, although they know that swimmers continue to access the increasingly dangerous cliff dives.

On the way down, I start to feel sick to my stomach. It isn't until we reach the bottom that I recognise this nausea as fear. There are younger teens at the bottom – boys and girls – sitting around a fire that has long been extinguished, drinking cans of cheap beer and cider, and executing the odd jump. It is both the best and worst possible place to be drinking as a teen. It is practically inaccessible by adults; I couldn't imagine the Gardaí making the long walk and abseil to take a few names. But the mixture of youth, alcohol, cliffs and the sea is a potentially deadly combination. The mood of the spot is laden with testosterone, and lads with varied diving experience, including none whatsoever, are being egged on over the edge.

We watch as three take their time weighing up height and safety, and pushing against the fear. The first two jump up and out successfully. The third goes weak-kneed at the last second as he steps over the precipice. A silence falls as he drops down instead of out, landing a mere six inches away from the rocky outcrop below, six inches from paralysis or worse. The others joke and slag him as he comes out of the water, and Michael and I try to explain to him how close he'd come.

Nothing about the place is safe: the passage to the cliff, the diving spots themselves, or the points of exit. Another, on coming out of the water, had bloodied his leg and torso. I won't be coming back here myself, and I advise against anyone else doing so given the state of disrepair it's in. I only wish I'd found it when I was fifteen.

To reintroduce a bit of calm in our lives, we return to Jameson's Pool where the super spring tide is still receding. We recline against the hot stone wall, reading our books, watching for the perfect level where the tide drops just below the wall, locking in the calm tidal pool. It is not as deep as it once was, having filled with sand over the years, and is perhaps five foot at its deepest point, though belly flops from the wall are still an option. A storm is needed to wash some of the sand away, or another whiskey merchant needed to dredge the sand or add a few more bricks to the wall.

Michael and I head back into the village, and then on to the Burrow Road, where an opening between a row of mansions brings you out onto an expansive and shallow beach. You'll be a while walking before you get to any depth at low tide. You could nearly walk all the way out to Ireland's Eye.

Earlier on, I met Patricia McCarthy, who has spent the greater part of her life overlooking the sea at Sutton Cross. 'Sometimes it's so beautiful, the sun is dancing on the ripples in the water. That calms you down. It's relaxing after a stressful day in town.' Pat was married to the late Jim McCarthy who won twenty-eight caps for the Irish rugby team, was a member of the Grand Slam-winning side of 1948 and toured with the first post-war Lions team in 1950. Jim spent the last three years of his life mostly confined to their home, with a view out the bay window overlooking the tip of Dollymount Strand. 'I used to say to him, "Look how lucky we are, sitting here, and every day is a different view." The light changes everything. Sometimes you think you could climb the Sugarloaf it's so clear.'

'I think it's in us all to hanker towards the water,' says Pat, 'because we came out of the water originally, there's a longing to be by the sea.'

HOWTH

Latitude: 53.361752
Longitude: -6.073814

Type: Bathing at Jameson's, distance swimming at Burrow Beach.

When: Perfect tide at Jameson's is an hour after high. Higher tides at Burrow Beach.

Access: As per p. 18

Safety: Jameson's Pool is not lifeguarded but is safe. Lifeguard at Burrow Beach.

Michael abseiling down to the Lion's Head.

3 Seapoint

Seapoint on a weekday is a workers' beach, loaded with commuters pre- and post-work. There are even workers who swim on their lunch break. So I decide to spend a full day at Seapoint to see who I meet. It's 6.25 a.m. and I spot a man in his fifties searching through a bin for something to eat. I pull an apple from my bag and offer it to him. He is much obliged.

'That's a very decent thing you did for that man,' says another fellow in his fifties with a temperate South Dublin accent and looking rather well-to-do. He has walked across the road in a fleece robe from the high-set Georgian terraces above. 'I sometimes come down with a cup of tea for him in the winter,' he says. 'It's terrible really.'

I explain that I'm supposed to meet a Finbarr here at 6.45. 'Well, I don't know any Finbarrs,' he says. 'There are some lovely people around here though, some real characters. You'd be chatting away to each other almost every day, though I have to admit, I wouldn't know their names. But you should talk to those two lads, they swim here every morning.' He points to two men wading in from the sea. As if to prove his previous statement, one of them turns out to be the Finbarr I'm after.

Finbarr and Joe are from Cork, but a long time living in Dublin. 'I'm full of auld talk,' says Finbarr. 'In November, when I go in to work and say to people that I've been in for a swim already, they're very impressed. They

View to Poolbeg chimneys from Seapoint.

assume I'm talking about a swimming pool. "No," I tell them, "the sea." Then they're even more impressed. But they don't know I've only got down for about ten seconds, in and out. I'll be found out one of these days. Me and Joe say ninety-five per cent of the benefit of swimming comes from having got out of the bed and come down.' Maybe they're right, though there's a lot to be said for the shock of the cold to get your motor running.

By 7.30 a.m. the sun is strong enough for factor 50. It's all men turning up: a couple of lads training for the Ironman competition next month, a man in his eighties jogging in squares of the beach at walking pace. It's surprisingly quiet for such a beautiful July morning, with only ten swimmers in the first hour. There must be loads of fibbers all over Dublin, bragging to their colleagues that they've been in for an early morning dip.

At 8.00 a.m. the place becomes busier, and for a little while it's all women arriving. I get in for my morning's swim now; the tide is on its way in but there's still a hundred yards of walking to be done before the water reaches my thighs. The DART whizzes by at more regular intervals and the sea starts to fill. A twelve-year-old boy explains to his dad, in a surprising level of detail, how the tides operate, the difference between spring and neap tides, the various angles of the moon to the sun.

A long walk for a swim when the tide is out.

At around 1.00 p.m., staff of the Front Line Defenders, a charity that protects human rights defenders at risk across the world, cycle down from their offices for a swim on their lunch break. I meet Louise, Ed and Michael. These three are members of an inner sanctum within the company: the Front Crawl Defenders, 'a call to armbands'.

The tide is high and the schools have broken for the summer. Hundreds of kids line the promenade and the water is busy with play. We find a spot for ourselves in the sea, shoot the breeze and throw a Frisbee back and forth. Some of their colleagues come down a little later in the hour for a breath of fresh air, including a Chinese member of staff – Irish alias Edward – who has also been in for a few dips this summer. I'm surprised to learn that he finds the cold as bearable as the next Irishman. 'There are lakes and rivers for people to swim in China,' he says, 'but nothing like this.'

Front Crawl Defenders play Frisbee on their lunchbreak.

SEAPOINT

Latitude: 53.297736
Longitude: -6.159613

Type: Bathing, distances swimming at marked buoys.

When: Better at high tide.

Access: Turn off Seapoint Avenue (N31) for the Martello tower.

Safety: Safe beach with lifeguard. Be careful of submerged rocks at high tides.

Above: Martello tower, Seapoint.
Below: The slipway below the Martello at Seapoint.

4 Forty Foot

Pat Rabbitte is on RTÉ Radio 1 as I drive towards the Forty Foot, speaking about his impending retirement from politics. He isn't planning on writing a book, anyway: 'Everyone has a book in them,' says Rabbitte, 'and that's probably the best place to keep it.' I drive on regardless.

I am on my way to meet artist and Aosdána member Gary Coyle. 'This is my 4,523rd swim at the Forty Foot,' he tells me as we swim together down towards the slip – a lesser-used exit point a couple of hundred metres south of the Forty Foot. Some sixteen years ago, in the spirit of the performance artist, he set himself the task of swimming at the Forty Foot every day for a year. Although he missed a few days that first year, he continues to swim at the Forty Foot and is, without doubt, a regular among regulars.

Scenes from the Forty Foot in Dún Laoghaire.

All eyes towards the next jumper from the rocky ledge at the Forty Foot.

Much of his work since has centred on the sea and his own seaside locality of Dún Laoghaire and Monkstown. The daily swim began as a joke on performance art, a form to which he could never relate. He brings a waterproof camera on each swim – a roll of thirty-six shots can last anywhere between four and thirty swims. For Gary, film equates to quality and encourages him to be sparing with what and when he shoots. For a period of four years, beginning in mid-2007, he collected water from the Irish Sea in various vessels and jars.

'I've stopped collecting the bottles of water now,' he tells me as we swim. 'It was driving my mother bananas.'

What he once thought of as an obsession has advanced a little further: 'After a couple of years, you start to realise this is a cult. If I went without a swim for three or four days I'd start to get withdrawal symptoms.' The resulting mood would be one of crankiness. Gary prefers to swim alone and likens swimming to meditation: 'It clears the mind completely, slows down the breathing.'

Gary has a detailed knowledge of the rocks above and below the waterline, mentioning names given to the landscape ('the Diamond' and 'Gladstone'). 'You'll see that an awful lot of the stone here was quarried. That's why you've a lot of straight edges. It was easier to drag the quarried rock onto a boat and ship it, rather than drag it up onto dry land using horses. They may even have used that stone for the Martello tower; both are granite. That was standard practice, to use the local material and work with what you had.'

He brings me close to the shoreline as we swim to take advantage of the warmth emanating from the rocks below. He also knows the intricacies of the water's flow: 'If you've a high tide here, the flow is southward, and if you've a really strong tide, like when there's a full moon and a full tide, you will shoot down towards Killiney. When the tide is low, the water is coming up the other way.'

There are photographs of swimmers at the Forty Foot dating back as far as 1843, and the Sandycove Bathers' Association has been in existence nearly as long. Gary bemoans the fact that they are no longer at the helm, since the council took over in 2014.

'This place was kept clean, everything was painted and weeded, they collected funds from the public and used it to maintain the place. And now because of insurance, the whole outfit has closed down. It was great because the men would stop people bringing in drink, ghetto blasters or dogs. Now, you come here in the summer and the character of the place has completely changed.'

Gary manages to steer clear of the inevitable politics, but is well versed in the transfer of management of the Forty Foot to the council. 'There were massive meetings and rows, of course. We can't have partial ownership. We still have the huts front and back, but that's it.' The land situated between

Sandycove and the Forty Foot is owned by the Manahans, who have been living here since the late 1950s. They also own the huts, and the Bathers' Association has come to an agreement with them to enjoy their continued use. And now that the Association allows full membership to women (since 2014, although pioneering women have been swimming here since the 1970s), they can now make full use of the huts for hot tea and shelter.

'I'm still only a young fella down here, and I'm fifty years of age. I got the key to the huts about five years ago. That's after ten or eleven years of swimming here. I was finally a made man! It's a big deal. I'd say there's only twenty keys max, and they change the locks regularly because people pass them on to friends.'

Our dry-land conversation which follows is interspliced with 'Cheers Donal,' and 'Hey Ronan, good afternoon, lovely water, I love your sunglasses. Down to the slip and back, gorgeous,' and 'Hi Richie, hi Jimmy.' All people Gary says hello to in the space of twenty minutes. 'I've loads of friends down here, I can come down any time of the day and there's always someone I know.'

In light of the council takeover, the presence of Tony and Dean at the Forty Foot, both working for Dún Laoghaire–Rathdown County Council, is sometimes contentious. But both are good-natured and chat openly with the swimmers.

'Are you not getting in?' Tony asks one of the onlookers. 'No, no, not here. I'm German,' she says, 'I'm not Irish enough.' I ask if they wouldn't go in

Michael and Brendan pose for the camera.

for a dip themselves. 'Sure, we were down here this morning testing the water,' they answer. 'Sorry about the temperature there,' they tell another swimmer, 'we had to turn off the immersion, council cutbacks.'

'One of the higher-ups is a year-round swimmer,' says Dean, 'so there's been a strong emphasis put on the maintenance of the spots managed from Seapoint up to Killiney Beach.' The brush that Tony scrubs the steps with is in a shocking state, missing the majority of its bristles. 'We'll put in for another one in next year's budget.'

They mention the raves in the cave at Whiterock further down the coastline. The cave itself had been fenced off in the name of health and safety, then opened with an angle grinder within twenty-four hours. 'Probably some gang had something hidden away,' Dean speculates. The cave stretches all the way up to the Witch's Hat at the top of Killiney Hill. As the two men finish, they are thanked by a lady emerging from the sea for bleaching the steps. They make it through another shift unscathed.

View from the rock ledge at the Forty Foot.

FORTY FOOT

Latitude: 53.289387
Longitude: -6.113811

Type: Bathing, distance-swims, jumping and diving, family.

When: High to low tide.

Access: Head for Sandycove Ave East or via Marine Parade (R831), heading for James Joyce (Martello) Tower.

Safety: See visual of submerged rocks posted. Safer swim around the corner at Sandycove.

5 Vico

Willie is enjoying a post-swim ciggy on the steps in front of the whitewashed shelter. He's come up from Bray on the motorbike for an evening dip. It's after work on Friday and his mood is good. In the first few minutes of conversation, Willie, Michael and I cover all sorts of topics: AC/DC at Lansdowne Road, nude swimming at night-time, and the strange ability of fresh air to put you to sleep.

Beyond the realms of the swimming spot, and particularly so in the city, it's unusual to strike up a conversation with somebody simply because you happen to be sharing the same five square metres. But the common bond of the swim – the excitement or nerves beforehand, the natural endorphin high that follows – entices people to open up and share their lives.

All the while, sitting a little further away from us near the old bath, is a group of six adults, male and female, of varying ages. Despite the presence of an acoustic guitar and their circular seating arrangement, nobody is singing. In fact, all the time we're there only two are in conversation – a young man in his early thirties perhaps and an older man knocking on for sixty. The younger man's name is John. Let's call the other Herodotus. They're in a

Willie smokes a fag and enjoys the view.

The 'bath' at Vico Road, a shallow pool that is submerged at high tides.

heated debate about … well, it's difficult to discern what it's about, but snatches of the argument are carried to us on the breeze.

John: 'You talk about superficial facts! Well then, who invented Germany? You can't even call yourself a Prussian anymore, the place doesn't exist.'

Herodotus: 'I don't think you understand history. I understand the materialist conception of history. It's like looking at the sea. One wave is going this way, and another going that way. But you need to understand the currents beneath.'

This isolated swimming spot goes by the names Vico Rock, the Vico Baths, and also the name given to it by Dún Laoghaire–Rathdown County Council: Hawk Cliff. For simplicity's sake, I've come to call it simply the Vico. It is the last bastion of nude swimming in Dublin. Even a Google satellite image at full zoom shows two pink figures stretched out in the sun. Despite the limited space available, there are numerous nooks and crannies in which to find privacy to disrobe. On a hot day, when the place is busy, people climb up onto the roof of the concrete shelter to lay out their towels or deck chairs. At high tide, even at mid-tide, the water is deep enough for diving. A narrow concrete platform, to which a diving board had once been attached, remains.

'Usually I'd swim at the Forty Foot,' says Willie. 'I'd go down some nights and the water would be like glass. I used to swim around the corner at Sandycove. One time a seal popped up beside me, then swam beneath me and brushed off my leg. I only swim at the Forty Foot now.'

The Battle of the Vico rages on.

Herodotus: 'I'm not suspicious of the English at all. A whole nation isn't going around being suspicious of another nation.'

John: 'The material facts are that the Armada did not defeat the English … Laissez-faire was two hundred years later. I'm not going to sit here and listen to your vague understanding of history.'

Willie, Michael and I talk about the sandy beach versus the rocky drop. We wonder aloud how there's any sand left on the beaches of Ireland given all the shoes that have walked sand into all the houses throughout the country over the years. Not to mention all the pockets that have collected sand over time, not to mention all the sand that's been washed out of all the heads of hair. Though admittedly, some of the latter sand makes its way home again via drainpipes.

The use of 'fuckin' and the frequency of 'my friend' increases as tempers flare between our two historians.

Herodotus: 'It's not philosophers who create the world: they interpret the world. They're a product of the material conditions of society.'

John: 'Do you know the reason why fascism couldn't work in England? Because England was a mixed-race society. Norman Anglo-Saxons didn't feel in union with their slaves, the Celts. That's why they think monarchy is so great.'

Willie allows us to take a few photos of him. 'My mate will kill me if the photo appears in the book,' he says, 'It's my first time ever swimming here and he comes here all the time.'

By this point, three of the circle of six have packed up and left. Two of them, rather awkwardly, are a middle-aged English couple who pass by with an embarrassed chuckle and an 'I think we'll leave them to it.' Eventually, the two interlocutors come to an impasse.

John: 'That's history, man.'

Herodotus: 'No, that's not history, John.'

VICO

Latitude: 53.269076
Longitude: -6.09778

Type: Bathing.

When: Easier access and exit from sea at higher tides, though doable at low tide.

Access: On the Vico Road, about 150m south of the Coliemore Road, there is a break in the wall. Follow the path that leads to a footbridge over the DART line.

Safety: Beware of submerged rocks at lower tides if jumping in. Also, difficult exit from water at low tide.

Vico swimming area and 'bath'.

2

Dog digging at Magheramore Beach.

6 Magheramore

Y ou'd pass the place easily, 1.5km south of Blainroe Golf Club. It's noticeable only by a couple of cars parked on the road. A large steel barrier blocks the entrance for cars as well as caravans and trailers. (I heard later that the owners of a tiny smattering of houses along the laneway wished to keep the beach to themselves but ultimately and, thankfully for the rest of us, lost that legal battle.) Michael and I trek down the picturesque, tree-lined avenue only to be stopped by a herd of cattle being moved from one field to another. At the end of the avenue is a tarmacked parking space in the process of being reclaimed by grass and moss.

On the beach we find the corpse of a baby whale, its black matte skin a giveaway. Its eyes have been taken by birds but the rest of the corpse is intact, not twenty-four hours washed up on the beach.

We've found that if you hang around a swimming spot for no more than half an hour, something will happen: a chance meeting, a conversation struck, some activity in the water – human or otherwise. So we lope around waiting for some action, but on a beach like this, you might prefer things to stay as they are: peaceful. The only sound is the gushing of waves. A high wall of lush reeds, fern and evergreens surrounds the beach, blocking out the world.

We disrobe and wade in; the thrill of the swim bites. Even the gentlest of waves raise laughter and screeching from the pair of us. Michael is trialling

Both photographs above: Magheramore Beach, County Wicklow.

View of Magheramore Beach from above.

his new toy, a waterproof digital camera. We have just about finished our swim when Michael spots a seal stirring behind us. I swim towards it and it ducks down and reappears a few metres further away. Then we turn back and it sidles up behind us. Each time we get close it moves away, and each time we move away, it comes closer. We play this game for a couple of minutes until it disappears altogether.

A passing couple on the beach tell us that the seal had been watching us from a distance, ever since we got in. Another swimmer, John, stops for a chat. We talk of the many swimming spots between Skerries and Curracloe; he has a good knowledge of the east coast.

He tells us that the nuns used to have a house up above on the other side of 'the low road', the R750 from Wicklow town. This beach was, he says, 'semi-private'. What does that mean in legal terms? It meant that the beach was public property, as it is now, but the nuns would have preferred you weren't there. There are plenty more Nuns' Beaches and Nuns' Coves along the Irish coastline. The land between the main road and Magheramore Beach is farmland. I ask John about access to the nearby beach behind Blainroe Golf Club. 'Well, they're not advertising it, are they? There are no signs that say "Beach Here". But there are no signs saying "Private Property" or "No Access" either. I'd say don't go asking questions, because you're unlikely to get the answer you're looking for.'

Michael and I head back to the car for tea and biscuits, and to write up some notes. Half an hour passes and the sun reappears. It's low set and the light is stunning. We agree to wander back down through the sunlit tunnel of trees for a few more photos.

Behind our backs, the metal barriers have been opened and the beach has come alive. About thirty kids are in the water, surfing on 2ft waves, producing the stuff of nostalgia for all the years ahead of them, their parents ensuring our continued connection with and respect for the sea.

Young surfers bring the beach to life in the early evening.

MAGHERAMORE

Latitude: 52.931082
Longitude: -6.02289

Type: Bathing, distance swim.

When: High to low tide.

Access: Off R750 at Magheramore, 1.5km beyond Wicklow town and a five-minute walk.

Safety: No lifeguard but appears to be a safe beach.

7 Brittas Bay

What's this, a weever fish? Would you stop the lights! Another cause for concern – this on top of being stung by a jellyfish or being dragged out to sea by a malevolent current. Lifeguards Luke and Ross are on patrol. Luke is about to begin engineering at University College Dublin, points pending. And Ross is about to start his Leaving Cert year. For the summer, however, both are entrusted with the safety of swimmers on Brittas Bay's north beach.

Wild flowers in the dunes behind Brittas Bay.

The most common issue they deal with is the weever fish sting. The name 'weever' derives from the old northern French word *wivre*, which comes from the Latin *vipera* meaning viper, adder or asp. Weever fish bury themselves just below the sand with only their eyes showing above water. The venomous spines on their front dorsal fin inflict excruciating pain on those unlucky enough to step on them. The poison is a protein that can be broken down by steeping the wound in hot water, 'as hot as you can take it,' says Luke. This also helps to soften the skin if the fin needs to be removed with tweezers. 'We've brought grown men to tears,' says Ross with a wicked smile.

We ask the lads about any other dangers on the beach. 'The current here is lateral,' says Ross, 'which means you're only going

Ross and Luke patrol the northern end of the beach.

to get dragged up or down the beach depending on the tide' – rather than straight out into the Irish Sea. That fact, along with the sandbank just beyond the shoreline, makes it a safe place to swim.

Michael and I take a long walk up the 6km stretch of beach. The sand dunes here are ideal for jumping and I can't stop reliving the long evenings spent executing ever more daring jumps with my brother on the dunes of Ballinskelligs in Kerry. I've a longer and heavier body than I did in those heady days of Club Orange and 50p pool games, but I warm up to the challenge and press my new daddy, Michael, to take a few mid-flight snaps. The photographs of my pitiful efforts, as you can see, didn't make the cut.

We continue walking in silence and my thoughts are still with my childhood holidays, the music that played on the radio as we drove through town after town, so many of them bypassed now. I had a full and happy childhood, but at seventeen years of age Ross and Luke are working away on the beach and in their spare time they race with the Wicklow sea-swimming club. They travel the country to compete in surfboard rescue competitions, a growing sport among young, strong swimmers. At their age, I was proving myself with straight naggins of Jameson and loafing around on a low-set wall at the edges of suburban Dublin. And while I managed to get through college and find respectable employment, my downtime was mostly lost to alcohol, an inevitable sex drive and other hedonistic pursuits. The energy of our teens and twenties can be spent in innumerable ways, but it doesn't always find the right outlet.

The hours of our lives can also be lost to the ambition to get ahead, to coming home at 9 p.m. instead of 5 p.m., to working seven days instead of five, only to regret it in later years. On retirement, nobody looks back and wishes they'd spent more time at their desk.

So when we pass through this period of living intensely – whether it be a misspent youth or a misspent adulthood – we can take stock. The base to start from is the person we were before hormones or career ambition took over our lives – to return to the innocence and instinctiveness of childhood.

Both photographs above: Kids at play on sand and dunes.

There are moments, or even whole days, when we can revert to that person to rediscover unconscious pre-teen joys like the sea. So that was the walk.

We head back to the car for lunch. On the picnic bench we chuckle at some poor mug handing over €7.50 to the only show in town for three Styrofoam cups of tea. Scores of children queue for a minuscule bag of chips at €3 a pop and an additional 20c for sachets of ketchup. 'We should be tweeting pictures of that price board,' says Michael. 'Hashtag: outraged, hashtag: daylight robbery.'

We come back to the beach for our post-lunch, post-snooze swim. Busloads of kids have arrived from the city and are being corralled into formation: a game is in progress. Out come our cameras and the awkwardness that goes with a pair of men taking pictures of children at play, taking care not to be too invasive and avoid identifiable faces. (Later in the summer we'll have business cards that explain what we're up to.)

The swim is gorgeous, the sea temperature bearable, and it's still early July. The tide is fully in and we wade out of our depth slowly but surely, wakened from our summer daze. We are blown dry by a cool breeze when we emerge.

Back on shore, three boys are taking turns to dig a hole, deep enough that the youngest's head has disappeared from sight. The eldest is about fourteen and shouting at the other two: 'Get Dad to bring me my phone.' He is clearly the foreman and very proud of his work. He wants a picture for posterity. Michael sidles up beside him, 'Are you looking for a job with the Council?' 'Would I get one? God, I'd love that.' Bless the youth, I think to myself. Bless the work.

BRITTAS BAY

Latitude: 52.886523
Longitude: -6.055103

Type: Bathing, distance swim, family-friendly.

When: High to low tide.

Access: Car park off R750, €4 per day parking.

Safety: Safe, blue-flag beach. Two lifeguard stations.

Brendan finally takes to the sea.

Wexford

3

Wild flowers at Curracloe.

8 Curracloe

We arrive at Curracloe on a Thursday evening. I take a snooze in the car as Michael checks out the unlikely amusement arcade in the car park. Then we scout the beach together. But instead of sticking to our task of finding a suitable place to camp, we revel in the diversity of wild flowers growing up from the sand on the beach, and behind the miles and miles of dunes, the lighting perfect under a mackerel sky.

Selection of wild flowers behind the extensive dunes at Curracloe.

Michael enquires as to the legality or otherwise of camping in the dunes. 'It's not strictly allowed, but you'll be grand if it's just the night,' is the answer we get. Grand. We put off the hard work of pitching the tent and take to Nellie's for a pint, curry and chips. I relate to Michael the rare skill I learned while living in Oxford of drinking just the one pint, and we shoot some pool.

Playing in the dark green light hanging over the pool table, it takes us a few minutes to realise that we are surrounded by murals of Omaha Beach. Curracloe was the setting for the D-Day landing scene in the film *Saving Private Ryan*. One mural shows German Messerschmitt Bf 109s flying over the heads of US troops as they struggle towards the beach. However, no German planes flew over the beach that morning. Another portrays a beach scene with an unlikely wooden signpost inscribed with the word 'Battlefield', pointing soldiers in the direction of the battlefield in case they should get lost. Another shows Steven Spielberg and Tom Hanks. A rather confused version of events. We finish our pool game: Michael 2: Brendan 1.

We pitch our tent in the shelter of the dunes.

When we left for the pub at 7 p.m., a gang of surfers and paddle-boarders had arrived at the beach; they are only leaving on our return at 9 p.m. With so many surfers in the sea and so many boards hiked up on the roofs of cars on the road, I wonder if we are writing the wrong book. We pitch the tent in the shelter of the highest dune. There is still light enough in the sky to read by, and time enough for a beer.

The sound of the crashing waves puts me into a trance. There is a period up on the dunes when time seems to slow down. The pace of our lives has begun to ease, with hours spent prying into rock pools and nosing up to flowers. I'm starting to realise that the swim is really just a reason to bring us to the sea, to set our minds – even for a few hours each day – to a calmer beat. Quietening the racing mind, the heartbeat, the breathing. I set my book aside and tune in to the breaking waves.

Horses race in the early morning.

First light comes at 5.20 a.m. I am woken by Michael's snoring, though his rhythm is in time with the crashing waves, so it is easy enough to fall back asleep. We get up at 6 a.m. to take photos for ten or fifteen minutes, then go back to bed. I am woken again at 8 a.m. by what sounds like a train careering down the beach. 'Horses,' says Michael. 'I got a few photos earlier.'

I get up and go out for a wander. A woman of middle age is walking her dog and a man of middle age is walking his metal detector. Cheaper than the Lotto I suppose; perhaps he is looking for movie memorabilia.

A swim is called for, but first we pack the tent away into a bundle twice as large as the one we'd unwrapped. The sea is flat and the swim goes down like a hot cup of tea: the first signs of a mild addiction. The sea is getting warmer, easier to enter, and we are visited again by a lone seal. I take in a bar of soap, and my toothbrush and paste. Something I'd seen first at the Forty Foot and wondered at. I am going mad in the best possible way, fulfilling an idea of myself as a mild eccentric. If nothing else, my housemates back in Dublin will appreciate the time and electricity saved on my usual long showers.

After our swim, we jog part of the beach and hop on the spot like a pair of auld Victorians at their callisthenics, setting ourselves up for the day.

CURRACLOE

Latitude: 52.388335
Longitude: -6.362264

Type: Long beach, distance swim, family.

When: High to low tide.

Access: Car park on the R743.

Safety: Safe, blue-flag beach. Lifeguard station near car park.

9 Baginbun

'At the creeks of Baginbun, Ireland was lost and won.' In 1170 two ships, the *Bagg* and the *Bunn*, led by Norman commander Raymond le Gros, landed on the small peninsula today called Baginbun. Their mission was to amass new lands for a group of Welsh lords who had fallen out of favour with King Henry. Le Gros and his band of 100 men took on a much bigger army of Norsemen and Irishmen from Waterford, but le Gros prevailed. Strongbow, who had sent le Gros, joined them the following year, took Waterford and declared himself King of Leinster. Thus began the '800 years'.

Another channel crossing is being recounted when we arrive at the car park at Baginbun Beach. One of the Wexford Masters Openwater Swimming Club remembers his view from the crew boat of a North Channel relay swim. 'We got well stung by jellyfish, so we did – all over. We'd be up on the boat

View of the beach from above on a glorious day.

looking down at Denise swimming: "Ooh, she just missed that one ... Aah, she got that one ... Arghhhh, there she goes again.'" Head first into a smack of Lion's Mane, ubiquitous foes of the North Channel swimmer. 'Then you'd hear her shouting up at us, "FUCK!"' That sounds very unlike the Denise Underwood who so kindly invited us to swim alongside the Wexford Masters on a Friday evening in July.

Baginbun is just one of a number of coastal locations where this sea-swimming club sets out from; others include Curracloe and Carne. But Baginbun is a beautiful beach, and in the right weather looks tropical.

However, it was Hickey's Pool, a small rock pool opposite the Martello tower on the headland, that brought the area to our attention. Anyone growing up or holidaying around Fethard, Carnivan or Baginbun will remember at one time or another taking the short cliff path to Hickey's Pool, where a previous owner, along with help from a group of locals, laid a set of concrete steps to provide access to the natural deepwater rock pool.

The current owners of the Martello tower seem less enamoured of swimmers seeking a dip in the pool. On the longer, western route, by Carnivan Beach, the closure of access is legitimate as the pathway would bring walkers onto their land. On the eastern side, there was a cliff walk leading to the pool that circumvented the tower. This pathway, which is still visible on satellite photos of the headland and on historical aerial shots of the peninsula, has been fenced off, and the thorny scrub and brush is so overgrown that the path is impassable.

There are mixed opinions among the Wexford Masters as to the right of access. Someone points out that the pool itself is below high tide and therefore cannot be in private ownership. We also talk about another Martello tower in private ownership: the tower in Bray that Bono once owned, but had to move out of because the glass rooftop turned the house into an oven during the summer months. Now he lives in a larger house with a view of the sea that inspired him to name a recent album *No Line on the Horizon*. It seems odd that any of the Martello towers are in private ownership, but there are only so many museums you can open in small coastal towns.

Back on Baginbun Beach, just before we set off for our swim, there is a bit of banter aimed at the three or four people not wearing wetsuits. 'Ye can't be putting the towel around your shoulders,' one swimmer joshes. 'If you're not going to suit up, you can't enjoy the luxury of a warm towel.' The slagging would usually come from the opposing side, with the skins accusing the suits of a lack of hardiness.

A German named Heidi is directing the gathering swimmers. While Denise directs the club on land, Heidi is the natural and uncontested leader in the sea. One of the lads informs me that 'she was some kind of serious swimmer back in Germany,' though his knowledge doesn't extend any further. The mystery only adds to the aura of authority. 'Let's make up one slow group and two fast,' Heidi says.

We set out for the tip of the headland, about 350m, and stop where the waters became rough. 'If you're ever swimming in the open sea,' Heidi advises, 'you need a kayak or a boat with you.' Duly noted.

I had opted for the slow group but, out at sea, I find myself somewhere in the middle. The first two groups set out quickly but soon all three groups merge. We stop at various points on our route to wait until everyone is accounted for. The heavens open, which comes as a welcome surprise.

Wexford Masters lead a swim off Baginbun beach.

In wetsuit or not, once you're this wet, you can't get any wetter and it's a novelty to be able to take such joy from the rain. I am surprised to find that some of the swimmers, even those in wetsuits, are finding the water cold.

It boosts my confidence to swim as part of a group where you get a sense of your speed and direction, or lack thereof, and the welcome feeling of safety in numbers. Back at the car park, a treasure trove of cakes, buns, tea and coffee is unveiled. 'This is the real reason why we swim,' we're told. 'You can eat what you like.'

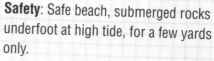

BAGINBUN

Latitude: 52.176461
Longitude: -6.830095

Type: Small beach, distance swim, family.

When: High to low tide.

Access: R734 south from Fethard. Short but slightly steep access on foot to beach from car park.

Safety: Safe beach, submerged rocks underfoot at high tide, for a few yards only.

Above: View from above, near the Martello tower. Below: Peter Bolger (left) and Enda Sinnott (right) of the Wexford Masters.

10 The Hook

Dropping down from New Ross and out along Hook Head we pass Ireland's 'most haunted house', Loftus Hall, where the presence of the auld divil and the ghost of a young woman have now been repackaged for tourists with an entry fee of €4. We turn left for Slade Harbour where the fishing boats are few and far between, yet hundreds of lobster pots are neatly stacked along the harbour walls and those of the ruined fifteenth-century castle.

An opening at the end of the harbour wall marks the beginning of the 2.5km walk from Slade Harbour to Hook Lighthouse. Michael and I set out looking for the distinctive overhang of rock that I've seen in images online, images that set your thoughts racing to fairy pools and nymphs sprawled out on rocks. After only 300m we find the rock pool-cum-grotto known as

Brendan takes a leap of faith into Solomon's Hole with Michael looking on.

Solomon's Hole. Smiles light up on our faces: we know we've hit on something spectacular.

As a rule, we only wear our wetsuits on longer swims, but seeing what we have found, we want to stay in for as long as possible before the tide recedes, so on goes the neoprene. We enter at the shallow end of the pool first, to gauge the depth and find our exit point. At full tide, the water rushes all the way into the back of the pool where horizontal dives (also known as bellyflops) can be executed from steps in the pool wall. Solomon's Hole is an incredible multi-tiered pool with a large rocky shelf that overhangs the water. A deep, narrow gully in the rock brings water in from the sea. The whereabouts of the gully is obvious when looking down from the best jumping point on the seaward side: the sunshine catches the pale shallow rock but doesn't penetrate the navy blue depths of the gully. Aim for that dark depth. This crevice in the rock is 12m deep so there's no chance of hitting the bottom, but it's only about 1.5m wide so be sure to hit your mark. And bring a pair of goggles for a chance to see crab, lobster or wrasse.

On the far side of the gully, a fisherman casts his line out to sea but my efforts to talk to him are hindered by a language barrier. He is Eastern

View of Solomon's Hole from above – too rough to swim that day.

Lobster pots at Slade Harbour.

European and happy as you like, seeking out early mackerel or pollock, though large fish and mammals inhabit these shores too. Whales and dolphins can be spotted from the headland with a good pair of binoculars. Otherwise a boat will take you out from Duncannon for a closer look at the fin, minke and humpback whales that visit in winter to feed on herring and sprat. Further along the coast we meet scuba divers who have been diving under the lighthouse in a deeper pool. There are other entry points along this stretch of coastline, such as Carraig Ahoy and Black Chan, but a field of rowdy-looking bullocks gives us a good excuse to turn back for a bite to eat.

THE HOOK

Latitude: 52.130925
Longitude: -6.908838

Type: Rocky jumps and dives, coasteering and sea-lounging.

When: Ideally high tide to an hour either side.

Access: End of Hook Peninsula, turn left for Slade. Walk 300m west from Slade Harbour.

Safety: Safe in calm waters. Use hard helmet, wetsuit and life jacket in choppy waters. Avoid in rough weather.

Waterford

4

Pier wall at Helvick Harbour.

(11) Portally Cove

'I like how all the animals are free,' Lisa remarks as we drive past fields of cows and sheep, 'until they get eaten.' Lisa is our photographer for this leg of the journey, and is also a vegan. She has prepared food in a series of small Tupperware boxes: carrots and hummus, seeds and nuts. She is surprised to learn that it isn't just beef cows that are out in the fields. Rather than being cooped up in a milking parlour, the milkers also roam free to graze the land. Until they get eaten, of course. Yes, dairy cows, when they stop producing, generally get turned into minced meat.

We have just driven from the nearby Ballymacaw Beach, where a small group of fishermen are about to plod over the hills for an angling competition, looking for pollock, wrasse and dogfish, and baiting with ragworm. They set off with large boxes-cum-seats strapped to their backs. They wonder at how

Approach to Portally Cove.

Both photographs above: swimming at Portally Cove. The dot, on right, is Brendan swimming out to sea.

and why we are living in Dublin. 'It's no place to live, man. Traffic, people, mayhem.' On this particularly sunny June day, out here by the sea, moving at the speed of melting ice cream, they seem to have a point.

We drive on another 4km to Portally Cove. The only thing going against it is the stony beach. The cove, as it appears from the winding pathway that leads to it, is breathtaking. The water is as flat as a lake, it being a narrow cove, sheltered on both sides for half a kilometre from the shore. I run back to the car for the wetsuit to make a good go of it.

I swim straight out towards the sea and get that wonderful, fearful sensation of being suspended over something dangerous, well out of my depth in an unknown and darkening body of water. After a couple of hundred metres I lie still on my back to see if there is any current or pull, to see which way I will drift. With no current, I press on towards the mouth of the sea, past gannets drying their wings in the sun, and say hello to oystercatchers prying between rocks. For a more experienced swimmer the open sea would have been manageable on a day like today, but I turn back as the waves are picking up, and the sailboats setting out from the marina at Dunmore East are coming into view.

Back at the beach, a young couple, newly married, have come in for a swim. The woman is having trouble coaxing her husband to get wet above the

PORTALLY COVE

Latitude: 52.139549
Longitude: -7.016498

Type: Small, stony beach.

When: High to low tide.

Access: Continue on R648 from Dunmore East or L4068, take byway due south at Portally.

Safety: Calm, safe beach. No lifeguard station.

Spot the hedgehog.

waist. He wades around for a long time, punishing himself, before he takes the plunge. And then they are both standing up, with their eyes focussed on a spot on the rocks just above the shoreline. Something is moving. A rat? A beaver? Not a curious seal this time, certainly. The couple saw it swimming only a moment ago, and now it is back on dry land but looking a little apprehensive. I tiptoe over the rocks and through seaweed to discover a hedgehog with its head buried into itself.

Perhaps it reflects poorly on me that my first instinct, and action, is to turn back for the camera. If the hedgehog has swum into this position, I reason, it can swim its way out. And to my later chagrin, I leave the hedgehog there. In hindsight, I feel like calling the ISPCA to have them confirm that I was right to leave nature well alone.

Back at the car we are ready to set off when the couple arrive up the hill, carefully minding a towel bundled up in their arms. The husband has rescued the hedgehog and is taking it home to release in their Waterford garden. An ideal practice baby. Lisa is pleased at another animal saved. I tip my hat to all vegans, but until someone invents a dairy-free 99, I'm out.

12 Guillamene

Lisa is still with us as we make our way across into Waterford. Kenny Cunningham and Brian Kerr are 'bigging up' the Ireland–Scotland match on RTÉ Radio 1 while George Hamilton enjoys a change of pace over on Lyric FM, rolling out the classical tunes. The distinctive smell of jam and porridge drifts from strawberry beds as we drive through Wexford to reach Guillamene just beyond Tramore.

I am developing the ability to read road signs backwards in the rearview mirror, so that I can tell immediately when I've missed a turn. When we finally arrive, three men are huddled round the diving board with a roll of gaffer tape. 'Just a bit of maintenance,' they explain. They seem trustworthy so I take a couple of springy 20ft jumps. The water is still plenty deep at low tide.

Diving boards are now few and far between along Ireland's coastline. An increasingly litigious culture means that town and county councils are less likely to install them. We will later learn that the lower springboards at Salthill in Galway are broken and waiting to be replaced. The two diving boards at Newfoundout, just beside the Pollock Holes in County Clare, are not *in situ* either; apparently the council ordered the wrong kind of boards

View of the Guillamene from above.

Brendan executes a dive from the steps.

from the US. They bought pool boards rather than sea boards, much to the consternation of local swimmers. Had we completed this trip thirty years ago we would have met with diving boards at Skerries, the Vico and numerous other places along the coastline.

However, the Newtown and Guillamene Swimming Club has done great work to keep its house in order, including raising funds for a new diving board in 2012 (the previous one having been broken by five men who took to the board simultaneously). The funds raised by the club paid not just for the installation of a new board but a vast amount of concrete and railing work as well.

The club also organises a charity swim each Christmas as well as the Snámh Fada and various swimming and diving galas. It also carries out cleaning and maintenance work with the help of the council. It appears to be working with the council, unlike at the Forty Foot in Dublin where the Sandycove Bathers' Association was forced to relinquish complete control of the swimming area it had stewarded since the 1880s. Like the Sandycove

Bathers, the Newtown and Guillamene Swimming Club is steeped in politics. Divided opinion over the addition and appearance of the railings and steps led to various letters to the editor and a Facebook campaign which showed the strong and very personal connection swimmers have to their spot.

Guillamene attracts scores of daily swimmers and there are plenty of dippers in fine fettle when we arrive in glorious sunshine. 'It gets warm eventually,' one swimmer tells us. 'Just give it twenty minutes or so.'

The water here is notoriously cold but beautifully clear. Deep water along an exposed stretch of coastline makes for an enticingly rich, green sea. A build-up of algae on the lower steps, often covered by the tide, makes entry here a little tricky but there are plenty of safe access points for the less sure-footed. A railing-free experience is available a couple of hundred metres away at Newtown, another favourite spot but one limited to high-tide swimming.

Brendan and Michael drying off at the Guillamene.

GUILLAMENE

Latitude: 52.143847
Longitude: -7.164886

Type: Bathing area with diving board.

When: High to low tide.

Access: Turn off the R675 for Newtown Cove and stay left at Y-junction for Newtown Woods, then left onto Newtown Glen.

Safety: Common sense should prevail. Ask and respect local swimmers.

Above: Jolly gents after a swim.

Below: View to Newtown Cove from above the Guillamene, tide out.

13 Helvick Cove

We put out a call on Twitter the night before that we'll be at Helvick Cove, at the unlikely time of half past three on a Thursday afternoon. We are in need of a local guide, as our plan is to head out from the cove and swim along the headland, a series of fractured sea stacks. We've no knowledge of the rocks below, the currents or pulls; we barely know what the tide is doing. We wait in hope for a response.

The weather doesn't know what it is doing with itself either. As we approach Dungarvan it seems like we are heading into a vortex. A dark, swirling mass of cloud hangs just above the Helvick Peninsula. Sean O'Rourke is on the radio, full of talk of killer seagulls, swooping down on sheep and stealing mobile phones from visitors to the Botanic Gardens in Dublin. The gulls are getting fatter and greedier. They'll be stealing goggles from the heads of swimmers next, plucking sunbathers up from their deckchairs.

Shelter to change and get dry at Helvick Cove.

Swimming towards the tip of Helvick Peninsula from the cove.

On the pier, hundreds of bloodied dogfish are racked up in boxes, their skin greying in the sun. The gulls won't touch them. Are they already full, or waiting for larger prey? Are they waiting for a mother to leave her infant unattended in a pram while she goes for ice cream? Yet another bad omen awaits us. Further along the pier we find a starling trapped in a lobster pot. We are ready to go and tell the king the sky is falling down. The bird flits about, trying to squeeze through the too-narrow netting. I reach a hand in but it flees from my grip. I call Michael over to take a closer look. I lift the lobster pot to get a better angle, only to realise the end of it is unlocked and the bird flies free. Then the clouds clear. We go back to the car park and soon a small gang emerges, six swimmers in all. We get some good information on the tidal pull and are warned not to go beyond a

More experienced swimmers back from a longer swim.

HELVICK COVE

Latitude: 52.054538
Longitude: -7.540001

Type: Small, partly stony beach. Distance swim to head or pier, family.

When: High to low tide, preferably high.

Access: Take R674 to the end of the road. Parking at pier only, walk to cove from there.

Safety: Safe swimming beside rock to or from pier, or out as far as the head. Turn back in choppy/open waters.

certain break in the rock. The water where we swim is flat as a cap, and I see my first starfish in Irish waters.

One of the swimmers we meet is Yvonne Whelan. She takes out her kayak, guides us up along the headland and tells us of her life since moving from Finglas, County Dublin, to Dungarvan twenty-three years ago. Brown crabs scrabble underfoot close to shore, and further along towards the headland, Michael, with his sea booties, is able scrabble up the barnacled rock face and dive back in.

Back at the cove, we regroup with the other swimmers. They have been on a longer swim, out to a buoy set in the middle of the bay. They speak of their training for the upcoming Dungarvan Bay swim, a fundraiser for the local RNLI lifeboat. All the signs of a healthy community are on display: coming together for strangers in a crisis, sharing local knowledge, providing good conversation and good craic. The same scenes take place across the swimming community, from Wexford to Cork, Kerry to Galway, right up to Donegal. As the man says, 'It'd be a great little country if you could only roof it.'

Cork

5

Michael entering the water at Garrettstown.

14 Myrtleville

Alarms for 5.15 a.m. Car for 5.30 a.m. Standing around in the rain for 6 a.m. Photoshoot 6.15 a.m. Swim 6.30 a.m. Hypothermia 7 a.m.

Let me back up a bit. When I heard we were meeting a crew of swimmers at 6.15 a.m., I had in mind a Forty Foot-style dip, a pre-work wetting to enliven the senses followed by flasks of delicious tea. I couldn't have been more wrong. We were among some serious swimmers. Liam Maher of Gabriel House B&B, who'd offered to put us up on the cheap, and had suggested in his original email that he was not a serious swimmer, is actually a beast of a man. Standing at 6 foot 6 inches and as broad as a bus, he's built for swimming: another English Channel solo swimmer. Where do these people get the energy, and the food?

The fifteen people who turn out for the morning's swim are all serious about their trade. James Slowey is training for the Norseman, a 226km uphill triathlon; Trevor Malone is training for an English Channel solo swim and, along with Ken, Liam and Carol, has completed the Lake Zurich swim. Michael and I thought we were just going for a dip. We are in training for a breakfast back at the B&B, looking forward to picking our eggs from

Back row (l–r): Trevor Malone, Liam Maher, Eddie Irwin, Denis Condon, Damian O'Neill, James Slowey, Jim Shalloe, Anthony Sloman and Ken Rodgers.
Front row (l–r): Carol Cashell, Brenda Sisk, Audrey Burkley, Brendan, Michael and Adrian Healy.

Adrian Healy, Eddie Irwin and Trevor Malone pointing with pride to their Sandycove hats.

Myrtleville Beach.

Brendan and Denis at sea.

the henhouse in the garden. I've brought only a pair of togs. Thankfully, we are given a set of Myrtleville club hats. In we get, and swim we do, brushing off harmless jellyfish as we go. This is a less horrifying experience than we expect. We are out of our depth soon enough and swimming for Dutchman Rock with dogfish cruising beneath us.

Not far from us is Fennell's Bay, which, I was told by a gent I'd met in a Dublin pub (me high as a kite, him drunk as a coot), had once been the reserve of Protestants. He was a reserved fellow himself. He later revealed that he was a Corkman but had adjusted his accent to Dublinese. He felt he'd had to in order to get ahead in business. He was fed up of the slagging.

Back to Myrtleville. I swim for twenty minutes, all in all. Long enough for the chill to penetrate my body, to cause me great difficulty in donning my jeans, or should I say more difficulty than usual, pulling all sorts of yoga poses to get my foot through each leg. I nearly stop the car on the drive back, I am so out of my senses.

The Myrtleville crowd have brought gallon bottles of warm water, ready to pour over their heads and bodies when they get out. One even has a plastic tray to stand in, so that the water gathers at his feet in a pool, which keeps his feet warm as he sits in his pull-out fisherman's chair. Bloody genius. Tea, muffins and sausage rolls, all home-made, are passed around the group. As a natural ascetic, I wish to take this opportunity to thank the better-prepared in life for sharing generously when people of my ilk realise their mistake.

Pre-swim jitters.

Heading out to the Dutchman Rock.

MYRTLEVILLE

Latitude: 51.782779
Longitude: -8.295182

Type: Small beach, distance swims and bathing.

When: High to low tide.

Access: From Cork city, head south on the N28 to Carrigaline. Beyond Carrigaline on the Crosshaven road, turn right onto the R612 for Myrtleville.

Safety: No lifeguard, but appears to be a safe beach.

15 Sandycove Island

We continue west to another swimming club stronghold on Cork's coastline. When Ned Denison got started at Sandycove in the early noughties, his sights were set solely on the 1,800m swim around Sandycove Island, an egg-shaped grassy mound that's home to about twenty feral goats. But some of Sandycove's regular island lappers weren't so sure. Who was this guy?

'It's a long way,' they told him. 'It's cold and it's half a mile long down the back. The waves are bashing against the rocks, you can't even come ashore.'

Little did they know that Ned had serious swimming credentials. He swam competitively as a kid in Vermont, and played water polo at club, university and national levels. Since then, Ned has swum the English Channel (35km), the Catalina Channel, California (34km), and the 'Round Jersey' swim off the coast of France (54km), to name just a few. Along with a cast of local and international swimmers living in and around Kinsale, Ned has turned Sandycove Island into an open-water swimming club of global repute.

'In the winter it was barren,' remembers Ned. 'On a shitty day there was two or three people; on a really nice day we'd have maybe ten. And the annual swim had maybe forty people at best.' So how has the group grown so quickly? 'Publishing a schedule was important,' says Ned. 'So was creating organised events. We also made people feel welcome.'

With us also is Mike Harris, an original Sandycove dipper turned distance swimmer. 'There were a few dinosaurs that had this anti-wetsuit thing,' Ned says, smiling at Mike, 'but they came around. The Thomond Swim when it restarted was togs only, and they had a really low turnout. Wetsuiters were very welcome at yesterday's Thomond Swim and they had eighty people.'

Along with Ned and Mike, Michael and I are joined for our swim by Carol Cashell, a pool swimmer who is ranked eighth in the world in her Masters age group at 1,500m. Carol transitioned from pool to sea first by completing the 2km Lee Swim, then making the leap to an 8km distance for her next race. 'The tears were pouring out of my goggles after the halfway mark. Swimming after a certain distance becomes a mental battle,' says Carol.

She has since swum Lake Zurich, a 26.4km race; is the fastest Irish person around Manhattan Island; and was the first person to swim around Bere Island in west Cork. Now she is preparing for the next adventure. 'There is always somewhere to swim. You constantly meet people at the swims, telling you stories of where they have been and what it was like. It gives you ideas of where to go next.'

Sandycove Island is an ideal training ground for distance swimmers, Carol explains. 'Conditions on the other side of the island are similar to what you'd get in the English Channel, though the water is colder. The Channel is 16 °C at the moment [26 July], it's 12 °C or 13 °C here – 14 °C on a sunny day. If you can tolerate this, then you can tolerate the Channel. And if you lap it and lap it and lap it, you know what mileage you're clocking up.'

'We've struck up a relationship with the local RNLI and harbour master too, and we give them feedback,' adds Carol. 'That's part of being involved in a group who are very conscious of where they're swimming; it's a public amenity at the end of the day. Swimmers are going to swim here no matter what so it's best to work together.'

'The harbour master put in yellow buoys,' adds Mike, 'which boats stay

Michael, Brendan, Mike Harris and Carol Cashell.

north of, giving swimmers a protected channel as they swim out around the island, with rope around the buoys for swimmers to hang on to.'

In addition to the welcome given to new swimmers, I ask what factors have led to the popularity of open-sea swimming at Sandycove in the past ten years. 'The popularity of the triathlon, and wetsuits,' says Ned. 'The disregard for speed, the emphasis on taking part,' adds Carol.

The Sandycove Island Swim Club describes itself as a club of convenience. There are no set training times, no official structure.

Mike tells the story of two brothers training for a triathlon. Both used suits. But one day, one of the brothers forgot his suit and so swam without. The next day, his taller, thinner brother tried the same thing. He got to the first corner and was completely out of gas. He crawled up onto the island and waited for someone in a kayak to bring him a wetsuit and give him a tow.

'The more surface area you have from which to lose heat, and the less mass you have from which to lose it, the quicker you will lose heat,' says

All in for a dip.

Michael chatting to Ned, Carol and Angela.

Mike, who is a retired cardiothoracic anaesthetist, and so knows more than most about anatomy and physiology. 'Long, thin arms and legs have a lot of surface, and skinny bodies don't have much of a core as a "heat sink". Thus a 175cm, 100kg pensioner like myself can swim daily for an hour at six degrees in February, by which time a 65kg, fit young runner the same height or taller would have been dead for some time. A tall, thin swimmer will have a large surface area through which to lose heat, and not far for that heat to travel outwards from the core, and will lose total body heat fast.' Below a core temperature of 35 °C, rational decisions and meaningful muscular effort go out the window. If you're getting that feeling of warmth and well-being when you know the water is cold, then get out, get dressed and get the tea down you. 'If you are involuntarily hyperventilating, have to get someone else to hold your teacup, and are shaking too much to stand on one leg to put your knickers on, then get fatter, get a wetsuit or don't stay in so long the next time,' says Mike. 'Or increase your stroke rate,' Ned adds.

With that, Michael and I suit up for a swim. Rough conditions on the far side of the island prevent us from attempting a circuit (though Ned has already set off in his Speedos). The rest of us take a route known locally as the 'pensioner's triangle' out to the island, back by an adjacent buoy, and ashore. The island itself is only 200m to 300m away, and we swim, stop and chat; swim, stop and chat. Looking back at the houses along the seafront, Carol, Mike and his daughter Angela, who has joined us, list the various people who live there and to what degree they, or their children, get in for a dip. More and more people from the local area are encouraged into the sea by the regular presence of the Sandycove swimmers.

Back on land, biscuits and tea are in abundance and, like the Myrtleville swimmers, both Carol and Mike have brought a gallon of warm water to pour over themselves.

The club is proud of its achievements. Ned says, 'At this point we have nineteen local English Channel swimmers. There must be forty Channel relayers. People swimming Zurich, Manhattan, Catalina, Gibraltar, whatever it might be. We've also had more than a hundred English Channel soloists swim around Sandycove Island. People have caught the distance bug. We are twenty years after the marathon-running bug and ten years after the Ironman bug. You can be the world's slowest swimmer, but if you just keep moving your arms, you will make it.'

SANDYCOVE ISLAND

Latitude: 51.677083
Longitude: -8.524004

Type: Concrete slipway into water, distance swims and bathing.

When: High to low tide.

Access: Take the R600 south of Kinsale, turn off onto the Ardkilly Ridge.

Safety: Safe on the lee side of the island. Discuss attempts to swim around the island with local swimmers first. Anticlockwise around island.

Above: View of the slipway at Sandycove. Below: Michael and Brendan arrive on Sandycove Island.

16 Garrettstown

My cousin Ronan Conway, shaker of hands and future Lord Mayor of Cork, had listed a number of places to swim in his home county. Like any Corkonian, he knows that Cork – city and county – is 'unbelievable, boy,' so his list was long, but Garrettstown was not to be missed.

The day after we swim here, he gives me a call to suggest that perhaps we shouldn't go cliff jumping at Garrettstown alone. But luckily, we were guided on our journey by GTown Surf School, situated at the east end of the beach. When the wind is low and the surf is down, they suit up and take to the cliffs for a stint of coasteering. Paddy is our guide for the next two hours. With an emphasis on safety, he shows us an incredible piece of coastline, with various caves, arches and rocky outcrops ideal for jumping from. The tide determines so much of what you can and can't do on any given trip, but every tide time has its own attractions. During our session we pass a 2m jump with a deep pool below, which over the course of two hours and a falling tide, turns into a 4m jump and a broken leg at the bottom.

GTown also provides helmets, wetsuits and an impact vest. Not a life jacket: an impact vest. But you'll need to bring a pair of old runners, which are absolutely essential for scrambling up, down and over the heavily striated rocks.

Paddy, Michael and I travel with a group of Austrian teenagers. 'There are two reasons I came to Ireland,' says Raphael. 'To be by the sea and to see caves. Now I've done both today.' As a souvenir, he takes home a long piece of kelp strangely similar to a multi-tasselled flogging whip. 'Can you eat it?' he asks Paddy. 'Oh, yeah, of course you can.' Raphael seems pleased with this. 'It'd be absolutely disgusting though,' adds Paddy, and we all crack up.

We are now a third of the way along our journey, and more and more are realising the importance of having a local swimmer to guide us, or even quizzing a nearby stranger who is drying off about the dos and don'ts for that particular spot. Unless you're swimming at a beach with lifeguards on duty, it is always worthwhile researching the area you're about to swim.

Making our way
along the coastline
at Garrettstown.

This is even more important when you are jumping into water from a rocky outcrop. You need to know the water depths, best exit points (or if there are any), swells and tides that might cut you off. Each spot will have its own quirks so find out as much as you can. With someone in the know taking care of our safety and sussing out each jump before we leap, we are free to relax and enjoy the experience. The scariest part is climbing across the rocks with an earful of water, which puts you off balance.

Paddy points to a large hole in the cliff that sounds like it was named after a cheap cider – the Devil's Hole – though it is only jumpable at really high spring tides. Other features of the coastal tour include the No Light Tunnel, Rocky Bay, the Blue Arch and Shark Rock.

All of the instructors are surfers and qualified lifeguards with years of experience in the water. 'When you're teaching a surf class, you stand around in the water for two hours watching everyone else having fun. Then when you're finished, you're dying to get in and surf yourself, but by that time the waves have usually died. Coasteering is great because you get to do exactly what everyone else is doing. And the tide is always changing, so you're taking different routes each time. It keeps it interesting.'

Is coasteering swimming? I hear you ask. Well, you can do coasteering even if you're not able to swim. All you need to do is to float (which will happen anyway because you'll have an impact vest) and flap your arms around a bit. So perhaps not. But it does involve getting from A to B through the sea and jumping off some tame and some tall cliff edges, so we couldn't say no.

Pádraig Burke crashes into the water from a height.

If coasteering in the south-east, contact Shielbaggan OEC; in the west contact Real Adventures Connemara; in the north-west, contact Wavesweeper.

GARRETTSTOWN

Latitude: 51.643711
Longitude: -8.58507

Type: Beach for swimming and surfing, rocks run for a kilometre or two from the western end of the beach.

When: High to low tide.

Access: Head south through Kinsale, cross the Bandon River heading for Ballinspittle. Turn off on the R604 for Garrylucas.

Safety: Common sense should prevail. Ask and respect local swimmers.

17 Lough Hyne

You may be wondering what a lake is doing in among all these coastal swims. Indeed, we were sticking strictly to sea swims. But Lough Hyne, for the last four millennia, has been a marine lake. The rising tide pushes salt water through a narrow gap so it mingles with a freshwater lake fed by a mountain stream. Lough Hyne became Europe's first marine nature reserve in 1981.

The other reason why we are ever so slightly bending the rules to swim here is the rapids. As the tides rise and fall, water pours in and out of the lake through a narrow gap. Twice in every tide cycle (twelve hours, twenty-five minutes), both the depth and the speed of flow are perfect for a bit of white-water body rafting. Calculating exactly when these two occasions in the cycle will occur is another matter. If the tide is too high the flow will be minimal. If the tide is too low your arse will be torn to shreds by the barnacles and rocks beneath. Our guide for the day is Steve Black, once a Sandycove Island swimmer, who breaks the disappointing news that we've arrived too late for the ideal tidal flow for the rapids, which happens about ninety minutes before or after high tide.

I am surprised to hear that the route to the rapids involves a 1,600m round trip. The lack of rapids and the relatively long journey out aside,

Swimming back from the rapids at the far end of Lough Hyne.

Steve's enthusiasm for Lough Hyne and for sea swimming generally gets us in the water. Off we set at a steady pace, but after about 200m of front crawl, I am keen to get back to the comfortable breaststroke. We stop mid-swim for a chat. Steve explains that breaststroke is bad for your knees, hips, back and shoulders.

But I find myself more out of breath during front crawl and less in control of my breathing – more likely to take a lungful of water on each breath. This is a common enough complaint and Steve identifies the issue. I am not relaxing enough; I'm trying too hard. 'Try five strokes instead of three before turning to breathe, it will force you to relax and slow down.' We reach the rapids, and I am glad we have come with someone who knows the lake well. It is deep, but generally safe. However, if you're swimming towards the rapids with an outflowing tide, you might get pulled over shallow rocky water. Again, think arse and barnacles.

Steve is a founding member of the Lough Hyne Lappers. 'People have been coming here to practise distance swimming for the past ten or twelve years,' says Steve. 'If the sea is dangerous or just plain miserable, people can come here to train – it's never rough.' We bump into one of the relative newcomers to the Lappers. 'Sean has gone from a novice to doing the Strait of Gibraltar

Paddle-boarders take advantage of the calm waters.

[10.5 miles/16.9km] in just three years.' Sean fills a plastic container with lake water and seaweed, then loads it into the boot of his car. His son has sprained his ankle during football and has requested the healing waters for a footbath.

There is a famous swimmer among the Lappers: Steve Redmond, a legendary open-water competitor. Redmond met Steve Black and Ned Denison seven summers ago. 'I understand you guys swim a bit,' he said, 'I'd like to learn.' Redmond had done his first Ironman but had breaststroked all the way. He was last out of the water.

'So what are your aspirations?' asked Ned. What they didn't know was that Redmond had signed up to swim the English Channel the following year. Ned thought Redmond was crazy but Steve Black offered him a few pointers. 'And he went off and did the slowest Irish crossing at the time, twenty hours and six minutes.'

The rest is history: Redmond went on to become the first person in the world to swim the Ocean's Seven (the English Channel, North Channel, Strait of Gibraltar, Catalina Channel in California, Cook Strait in New Zealand, Molokai Channel in Hawaii and the Tsugaru Channel in Japan).

I want to know what is so special about Redmond that makes him able for the Ocean's Seven. 'Mental toughness,' says Steve. 'He is tenacious. I would imagine he has a low heart rate. And he's the most unassuming, nonchalant guy you'll ever meet.'

While chatting to Steve Black, I try to take advantage of his swimming knowledge. What makes for a good swimmer generally? 'You must learn to be efficient, to not waste energy. Get the right stroke rate and learn how to change your stroke rate according to the conditions. Know how to swim low in the water,' Steve advises. 'I tell people to swim "downhill" in the water when the conditions are rough. Redmond was a blank canvas so it was easier with him. Everything you told him to do, he did. He didn't have any preconceived ideas or bad habits to get rid of. If you saw him swimming now, he could swim forever.'

A drive over the hills.

The northern end of the lake.

Under the sea.

The Lappers swim here every Tuesday, Thursday and Sunday. 'If you follow the shore all the way around it's two miles so you know your distance,' says Steve. It's a testament to their openness and friendliness that you can come and join some of the legends of Irish open-sea swimming and get a few tips from them if you're willing to learn. Steve doesn't suffer fools. 'Life's too short for doing things you don't enjoy, so if you're going to be moaning about the cold, then just don't do it.'

LOUGH HYNE

Latitude: 51.506075
Longitude: -9.303937

Type: Tidal lake, distance swims and bathing.

When: High to low tide.

Access: Come off the N71 and onto the R595 at Skibbereen. Lough Hyne is on the Wild Atlantic Way.

Safety: Safe but deep lake.

18 Barleycove

The journey from Cork city to Barleycove is a long one. And we are making our journey longer by taking a detour through the townland of Kilbrittain, a rebel place name if ever there was one. On board the good ship Yaris is our dear friend Pádraig Burke who arrived in Cork this morning to guide us for the day. Paudie was born and raised in Kilbrittain, leaving as soon as he got the chance. He has spent the past twenty years studying and working in London, Belfast, Australia, and now Dublin.

We had been relying heavily on satnav till now, but Paudie takes us on various scenic routes as we cut through west Cork. 'That's the famous statue of Our Lady,' Paudie points out as we drive through Ballinspittle. In July 1985, it appeared to move. In the weeks that followed hundreds of thousands of people converged on the town. On the way to Kilbrittain we pass through Courtmacsherry. 'A whale washed up on the beach in Courtmac years ago,' says Paudie, 'and Kilbrittain stole it from them, the feckers.'

Barleycove on a nicer day than the one we arrived on.

Braving the bad weather at Barleycove.

What he means by 'stole' doesn't become clear until we see the whale's skeleton sitting in a concrete enclosure fenced off with wire. You can slot a €2 coin into a machine that gives an audiovisual explanation of how it came to be there. It presumably doesn't explain that the whale was 'stolen'. Kilbrittain felt it could do with a new attraction and Courtmac had plenty going for it already, including a coastline. Local councillors and the Minister for the Environment were drawn into the argument, which eventually went Kilbrittain's way.

It is the first time Pádraig has been in Kilbrittain since his mother died three years ago. 'She was a great visitor of graves. She'd be mad at me now for not having visited.' He brings us by the local graveyard where we stop for five minutes. Michael and I stay in the car to read the Saturday paper.

Pádraig surveys the rubble of his childhood home.

Brendan catching a wave as well as the rain on his back.

Paudie takes us by the house in which he spent the first eighteen years of his life. Would he know who lives in all these houses, I ask, as we near his own. 'Oh, God, yeah. You'd know everyone who lives nearby.' In quick succession he lists off the names: 'That's Horgan's, that's Lordan's, that's Keohane's.' After a slight pause he adds in his casual, dark-humoured way, 'But sure they're all dead now.'

His childhood home is now a large pile of rubble. It is also the construction site for a new building, the foundations of a house his brother, the eldest son, is building. Pádraig is the third and final son of eight children. 'Like Michael Collins,' he tells us, another Corkman born not far from here.

He walks over the rubble, and from the remains of the wall below where his bedroom had been, he points out Kilbrittain Castle. The castle is no more than a mile away but he has never visited. We go up its long driveway to find a single Ford Focus parked in front of the castle. It's the oldest inhabited castle in Ireland, dating back as far as the eleventh century. From a distance it looks abandoned but it is apparently still lived in, a hotel until recently. It seems odd that such a grand estate, so physically near to Pádraig during his childhood, was so removed from his and others' experiences of the area.

Mother and son at Barleycove.

We take to the roads again, stopping to buy a sandwich and a losing Lotto ticket. We are heading for a late-evening swim at Barleycove, an edge-of-the-earth beach only about 5km from Mizen Head. I passed by it in the car last year in some rare February sunshine and imagined how it would look in the middle of July, packed to the rafters with swimmers and sunbathers.

Conversation in the car stretches from Pavarotti vs John McCormack singing 'The Kerry Dance' to the titillating place names of Cork's towns and villages: Belgooly, Reenascreena, Riverstick, Ballylickey and Snave (*Snámh*). But as we approach Barleycove, clouds gather and the rain unfurls. The roads are near empty. The car park is completely empty. It is Saturday night – anyone with any sense is already where they want to be: not at the beach.

We sit in the car and devise a plan: put the togs on and wear rain jackets over our bare skin. Race down to the beach over the floating bridge. The tide is out, however, and it's a longer run than we were expecting. By the time we arrive on the beach we're buzzing. Another long run to the water. Getting down into the relatively warm water is a great respite from the rain and wind lashing against our chests. We are delighted with ourselves, bursting into the waves with Paudie taking pictures from the shoreline. I run back to get the larger camera, and risk a few snaps in the crashing waves. It reminds me of similar swims in St Finian's Bay in Kerry as a kid. You've come away on holiday, a week of rain has kept you out of the water long enough, but it doesn't matter any more. You're going to get cold and wet and you may as well have a bit of craic.

A woman walking her dog stands in the rain and watches us. She passes on as we begin to clamber back over the dunes. Barleycove has some incredible foredunes, and a stream that wends its way towards the sea, creating a lagoon behind the dunes, and onwards into a wider river mouth that gently washes out to sea.

When we arrive back at the car park another car has arrived. It is stopping and starting, sputtering up and down the tarmac. A father is teaching his teenage daughter to drive. Michael makes eye contact with the father, makes a circle of his thumb and index fingers in a hopeful 'OK' sign. The father looks back at Michael and clasps his hands together in prayer. Paudie and Michael hold their hands in prayer too as we make our way back to the city along dark, winding roads through the driving rain.

BARLEYCOVE

Latitude: 51.472443
Longitude: -9.768203

Type: Large beach, swimming, bathing, family.

When: High to low tide.

Access: Follow the R591 for Mizen Head. Take a left over the narrow road that cuts over a lake for Dough.

Safety: Blue-flag beach with lifeguards on duty.

Kerry **6**

Boats at Meenogahane.

19 Derrynane

Bring your children to Derrynane Beach. If one of them turns into a psychopathic killer in later life, you can rest assured that it's not your fault. You gave them the opportunity to experience life at its best. I had just driven from the town of Ballinskelligs where I spent the happiest days of my childhood at St Finian's Bay and Ballinskelligs Beach. I'm the youngest child of five and now at the age of thirty-one, my family and I still spend the majority of our summer holidays there. My experiences of Ballinskelligs are undoubtedly why I've come to spend a summer chasing sand and sea around Ireland.

So it is hard to admit to myself that only half an hour's drive down the N70 is a far superior beach. There exists an alternative childhood even happier than the one I've experienced. What I could have achieved had we holidayed instead at Derrynane! I might have been a media mogul, a Buddhist monk or, perhaps, a better writer. Hannah and I park up and walk east, past sunbathers and children's construction sites, towards the rocky outcrop that splits the beach.

View of Derrynane Bay with the Skellig Rocks in the distance.

The water temperature rises as we walk towards the large black rocks, which have been warming in the sun all day. Now the tide is in and the rocks act like the element of a kettle, releasing their heat into the sea. The water is crystal clear and, wearing goggles, we weave among the shallows, spotting large and small fish, and crabs crawling across the seabed. For the second time in my life I am swimming through seaweed on purpose. For the first time in my life I am enjoying it. The sun is impossibly bright, illuminating the sometimes ominous-looking mysteries below.

On the western side of the beach twenty or so children line up on a pier, calling each other to dive in. The pier protrudes from a tiny beach in a small natural harbour, almost entirely enclosed by land, ensuring calm waters. A four-year-old boy is being coaxed to jump off the pier by his father who stands below him in the water, arms outstretched. Minutes pass as the little boy agonises over his decision at the water's edge. He bends his knees as if to pounce or even collapse into the water, his dad saying, 'Come on now, you

Derrynane Abbey.

Kids leap from the small pier on the western side of the beach.

91

View of Derrynane Bay and Abbey from the N70.

did it twice yesterday,' more for the sake of the onlookers who are pretending not to watch. 'But Dad,' says the boy, 'this isn't a very good life jacket, is it?'

A small girl with an ever-so-slightly turned-up nose, of cartoon imp appearance, approaches in her wetsuit covered by a dressing gown. She is maybe a year older but equally minute, no more than three and a half foot tall. She's not getting in, and is already dry but, encouraged by the boy's father, she eventually leaps from the pier. She returns to the boy's side soon after, trying to talk him into it. Despite the boy's wetsuit and life jacket, he's shivering. He shifts along the pier a few feet, worrying that the water isn't deep enough (indeed, he is probably right: the water is just above his dad's waist, and the tide is visibly receding as he delays).

Hannah and I can't watch any longer. We've taken an inordinate interest in the spectacle. We walk towards Abbey Island but keep craning back to watch as the boy continues to tilt his body forwards. He gains a greater following at the pier-side, all of whom are goading him on. We delay just long enough to see him walk back towards the beach with his head hanging. Perhaps he'll remember that moment all his life, that childhood nightmare. He'll become a procrastinator, blame his parents for all his future failings

DERRYNANE

Latitude: 51.759744
Longitude: -10.137613

Type: Bathing, distance swimming.

When: High to low tide.

Access: Off the N70 at Derrynane Beg or Caherdaniel, following winding roads towards the sea.

Safety: Blue-flag beach with lifeguard. Largest of the beaches on the east is known locally as Danger Beach due to rip tides.

German swimmer at Derrynane Abbey.

and humiliations, curse them for ever taking him to Derrynane Beach. Perhaps he should have gone to Ballinskelligs.

It's a very short walk to Abbey Island (more often a peninsula, except at high tide) where the remains of a sixth-century abbey are situated. We wind our way through gravestones, under archways, and read off the names of the dead as we go: Gradys, O'Sullivans, O'Connells – including Mary O'Connell, wife of Daniel, the Liberator. Their former home, Derrynane House, is set just behind the main beach in the 320-acre national park. The building itself is a public museum to Daniel O'Connell and his life. The cove where we watched the little boy on the pier was frequented by smugglers throughout the eighteenth century. Tea, brandy, butter, wool, salt and hides were bought and sold by Daniel's uncle, Maurice 'Hunting Cap' O'Connell, an industry on which he grew wealthy and afforded his nephew an education at King's Inns and a career in parliament.

The evening wears on but the sun continues to shine as bathers lounge in the shallows. Three middle-aged German men dive off the rocks in the shade of the graveyard. It seems fitting that such vital displays of life are overshadowed by reminders of the inevitable. What is it they say? 'Life's a beach and then you die.'

20 Dingle Lighthouse

We set out at noon from the beach at Binn Bán, not remembering how I'd come to know of a swimming spot below the Dingle Lighthouse. I am joined by my brother Conor and his fiancé, Steve, as we take the cliff walk and watch half a dozen boats circle the bay in search of Fungie the dolphin.

At low tide, we are disappointed to find the rocky inlet too shallow to jump into, with seaweed reaching to the water's surface. The lighthouse is under renovation but the views of the bay are unobstructed. Across the bay on Carhoo Hill is Eask Tower, a Famine Relief project built in 1847. The tower was built of solid stone, 5m wide and over 8m tall. The wooden hand protruding from the side of the tower signalled ships to let their sails down, allowing them time to lose speed before entering the blind mouth of the harbour. Many Famine Relief constructions provided no economic or structural benefit, and in the same spirit of inefficiency, this tower seems disproportionately tall and thick in comparison to its relatively minor function.

The same evening I return to the lighthouse alone, this time taking the turn-off for Kilnaglearagh. As I park up, the heavens open. Two sensible

Looking down on the two swimming ledges at low tide.
Inset: Steps below the Dingle Lighthouse leading down to the swim spot.

women of middle age are sheltering under the hull of a small fishing boat so I invite them in out of the rain. They talk to each other in Irish and to me in English. I am gently and rightly scolded for swimming alone. 'What if you hit your head off a rock?' they ask. I promise them I'll be extremely cautious. I ask them if it is true that the boats don't charge if their passengers don't see Fungie. 'Oh, they make sure you see him, even if it's just the fin. They celebrated his thirtieth birthday there last year. He's getting a bit daft in his old age,' they say. 'He doesn't interact as much either; he's not as playful.'

The rain clears. The two ladies offer to follow and watch me as I get in for a swim but I politely decline. I'm in a rush to be back for dinner with the family in Ballyferriter.

Hitting my head off a rock is very much on my mind as I undress. The wind is up, too. I feel very alone as I visualise by body drifting out to sea. But I'm careful to check my entry and exit, and I know from my earlier visit that there's plenty of depth now. A series of steps down the rocks leads to two concrete platforms from which to dive, but there are no steps leading out of the water, just heavily barnacled rocks to crawl up.

View from the coastal path near Binn Bán.

I'm drying off and in daydream mode when I see a small wooden boat with an outboard engine whirling in circles. Beside it, Fungie is diving like a mad loon, five or six jumps, right out of the water, each jump within a second or two of the next. Then all is quiet. A minute later, the same again.

As I walk back to the car, the boat teasing and coaxing Fungie to perform has lured him over to my side of the bay where a handful of tourists hang at the water's edge with cameras and binoculars in hand. The boatman is steering and taking photos all at once but Fungie is becoming worn out. He breaches the surface but there are no big leaps. Both Fungie and I lose interest and head off in our separate directions.

DINGLE LIGHTHOUSE

Latitude: 52.121419
Longitude: -10.258529

Type: Bathing.

When: High tide only.

Access: Set directly below the Dingle Lighthouse, along the cliff walk between Dingle and Binn Bán.

Safety: No lifeguard and tricky access out of the sea – confident and careful swimmers only.

Sheep leave their mark on the barbed wire.

21 Coumeenoole

Coumeenoole was to have been the main location for the 1970s epic film *Ryan's Daughter*. Indeed the beach is generously featured throughout the film but would have been more so were its waters not so bloody dangerous. In the opening scene, Rosy's (the main character) parasol is blown from the cliffs at Coumeenoole and lands in the currach of Father Hugh and Michael below. In the following scene the pair land the same boat nearly 10,000km away at Kommetjie Beach in South Africa.

What led cast and crew on a journey to shoot the only scene to be filmed outside Ireland? In the scene, Father Hugh (Trevor Howard) and Michael (John Mills) are coming in from a day's lobster potting. On location, their currach was tied to a pulley that towed them out and then in from beyond the breakers. On their first attempt, they were successfully pulled ashore, only to be knocked head over heels by an incoming wave.

View from the beach out to sea.

Coumeenoole Beach shot from the walkway leading down.

Their second attempt fared much worse. Take this passage from Michael Tanner's book on the making of the film, *Troubled Epic*: 'Coumeenoole is notorious for its eddies and cross currents; and on this particular morning the swell desired by [director] David Lean ultimately proved too strong. Watching locals shook their heads in disbelief at the thought of any fisherman braving the prevailing conditions, let alone two actors aged sixty-one and fifty-five, weighed down by costumes on top of wetsuits.'

As the currach was being pulled back ashore for a second time, a 20-foot breaker crashed over them, upturning the boat, with the gunwale delivering Mills a violent belt to the head. From the shore, Mills and Howard disappeared from view, presumed stuck beneath the upturned currach. But Lean told everyone to stay put: 'You'll ruin the sand,' he was heard to call. Eventually one of the divers on hand swam out and kicked a hole through the canvas of the currach and pulled Mills out. The scene was finally shot on a much calmer beach in South Africa, thought similar in appearance to Coumeenoole. All they had to do was paint the rocks black.

On the sunny, blustery day that I arrive, the waters are significantly safer. Signs warn against swimming, but that is not unusual nowadays at beaches or by rocks with a strong tradition of swimming. These waters must be respected, however. My rule for a beach like this is not to go beyond my waist in depth, though even that doesn't guarantee safety.

The setting is extraordinarily beautiful. Streams trickle down the face of the surrounding cliff; the water works its way quietly through the beach out to sea. The old track that led down to the beach is just about visible. On a sunny day, this small beach is tightly packed with people and gets tighter as the tide comes in. There is no lifeguard on duty, though on days like this there are enough willing bathers and boogie-boarders to merit one.

The water is cold but the energy expended on battling the waves keeps you warm, or acts as a good distraction at least. I always find it easier to walk into choppy waters; otherwise getting wet is too incremental and more painful than needs be. On the road in, Trá Bán on the Great Blasket seemed so close. In fact, it is only 5km away, but an exceedingly dangerous current between it and the mainland prevents even the strongest swimmers making the journey. The boats to the island have been called off for the next two days. Trá Bán is known for its cold waters, friendly seals and beautiful white sand.

I follow the swim with my first 99 ice cream since Tramore. How did it take this long, I wonder, though a post-swim latte and pastry from a roadside garage is becoming de rigueur as the journey progresses.

COUMEENOOLE

Latitude: 52.109257
Longitude: -10.463933

Type: Bathing, boogie-boarding.

When: High to low tide.

Access: On the R559, the coast road and the Wild Atlantic Way.

Safety: No lifeguard and not safe by any means. Some submerged rocks.

Left: A stream trickles down off the cliff onto the beach.

Boogie-boarders brave the water.

A seagull preens above the cliff.

22 Brandon Creek

t's mid-July and the sea is raw white with waves crashing just beyond the opening of Brandon Creek. Tour boats for the Skellig and Blasket Islands are tied up at port due to a small-craft warning from Met Éireann. The Beginish Island Swim, just off the coast of Valentia Island, has been cancelled. But in the narrow grip of the arms of Brandon Creek the water is relatively still.

It's 8.30 a.m. and a cool breeze is blowing. The sun is beginning to break open the clouds but not penetrating the high walls or the creek's deep waters. Even at high tide, there's still a decent jump off the pier at Brandon Creek. I have forgotten my goggles so a dark green blur is all I can see and my thoughts turn to lampreys. I only learned the day before about these bloodsucking eels, which attach their mouths to fish, and sometimes humans.

The water feels thick and heavy below me, bottomless almost; the morning is playing tricks with my mind. I swim to the fishing boat anchored in the creek and hoist myself over the gunwale to see what I can see: a lobster pot, a motor for pulling in line, a pink buoy; not the hoard of cocaine I am expecting.

Despite the ominous mood, it is a refreshing and enjoyable swim and the scenery above water level is beautiful. I later learn that fewer than half of the thirty-eight known species of lamprey are parasitic, and those that are only approach humans when starved.

A seafarer, and namesake, who was familiar with sea monsters is St Brendan, for whom this creek is named. St Brendan set out on his voyage

Brandon's Creek at sunset.

Pier at Brandon Creek with vessels old and new. A stream rolling down from Mount Brandon into the Creek.

across the Atlantic in the early sixth century from this very spot. It was also the departure point for historian and explorer Tim Severin, who aimed to replicate Brendan's voyage in every possible detail in 1976. The boat he captained was locally crafted – its hull of local ash and oak was covered in ox hide, tanned in water steeped with oak bark. The leather was sewn with threads of hand-rolled flax. All as recorded in the *Navigatio Sancti Brendani Abbatis* ('The Voyage of St Brendan the Abbot'). Severin's five-strong crew sailed more than 7,000km across the Atlantic in a 32ft replica medieval sailboat.

The 'Island of Sheep' and the 'Paradise of Birds' that St Brendan described are actually the Faroe Islands, where the Faroese also have a 'Brandon Creek' where he landed. Brendan's 'Land of Spewing Rocks' is akin to the hot springs and volcanoes of Iceland, and the heavy fogs that Severin encountered by the tip of Greenland are like those that Brendan recorded.

When Severin's team reached Newfoundland, they were greeted by the Wexford accents of the descendants of the country's many Irish settlers. Severin proved that Brendan's technical knowledge would have been sufficient to get there. There is evidence that Christopher Columbus worshipped in St Nicholas' Church in Galway in 1477. His main purpose, it is suggested, was to consult a copy of the *Navigatio* before setting sail for America.

I dry myself by a boat that could be a descendant of Brendan's – a fisherman's currach, its upturned canvas hull covered in crackling tar. I dream of greater voyages ahead and hot cups of sugary tea to wash down my breakfast.

Above and below: A breakfast dip at Brandon Creek.

BRANDON CREEK

Latitude: 52.237882
Longitude: -10.310336

Type: Bathing, swimming.

When: High tide for pier jumps.

Access: Between Ballycurrane and Ballinknockane, about 3km west of the summit of Mount Brandon.

Safety: No lifeguard, deep water around the pier. Check depths before jumping. Calm waters generally.

23 Meenogahane

John Edwards came to know Kerry from the passenger seat of a truck. He was on the road with his dad from a young age, delivering supplies to hotels and restaurants. 'My dad always seemed to take the long route,' says John. 'He wanted to see what was down every lane.' As a young surfer, John used this knowledge, trawling through his memory for byways that led to big surf.

'In my early twenties, when I started surfing in a big way, I was very curious to check out places and find new spots. We spent weekends on the road, sleeping in the backs of vans, poking around looking for surf spots. Not realising that I was building up this great knowledge of swim locations

Slip and wall at Meenogahane.

Good for a climb and a few jumps.   John jumps into a deep gully.

as well.' As he begins his new business, Wild Water Adventures, John's knowledge of Kerry's coastline pays off as he leads small groups to the county's best wild swimming locations.

'People are looking for places that are out of the way. They're looking for remoteness and wilderness, for natural beauty and cleanliness, and I think that's where Kerry really stands out.' John lists various lakes in the Conor Pass as well as wedge tombs and passage tombs.

But today he takes us north of Tralee to the little-known townland of Meenogahane. 'It's mostly locals swimming here. I discovered it when I was training as a diver.' Indeed it's a diver's paradise; even a pair of goggles will stand you in good stead. We swim under a sea arch and into a cave to experience the unusual sound of water breaking in a circle around us. We jump into a deep crevice from a shelf of rock and climb a sea stack for panoramic views. John and I switch seats as he jumps into the sea and I take to the kayak with the camera. This is an ideal place to bring adventurous, confident kids. It's a relatively small area and safe, but there's plenty to see.

'In my experience,' says John, 'you can't lose with swimmers. It might be raining and it might be a bit miserable, but when everyone comes out from the swim their faces are lit up. There's that natural high; the endorphins are buzzing.'

Places such as Meenogahane are lucky not to have been affected by the storms of recent years. As a winter surfer, John is more in touch with the changing of sands and rips than most. 'The big storms in February 2014 took a lot of sand hills away. Banna Strand hasn't really recovered, and new rips have appeared. Coumeenoole had a lot of sand taken away too, with more rock exposure now. And lots of shipwrecks have become exposed, which had been buried in sand for years.'

A couple of months back, John came down to a Mass taking place on the pier. He later learned it was to mark the centenary of the sinking of the *Lusitania*, torpedoed by a German U-boat. The ship went down off the Old Head of Kinsale but the bodies of four of the 1,198 who were killed drifted hundreds of kilometres north-west to the shore at Meenogahane.

John also remembers the story of a Danish ship wrecked in 1730 near Ballyheigue Castle, home to the Crosbies, a powerful Protestant family, who may have purposely lured the ship to wreck. Of the twelve chests of silver that were salvaged and stored in the castle, nine were taken in a raid, purportedly an inside job instigated by Lady Margaret Crosbie. (Sir Crosbie died soon after the wreck, allegedly poisoned by Lady Margaret. She claimed he had died due to exposure on the night they salvaged the wreck and sought damages of £4,300 for her loss. Crafty.)

As we head towards Fenit for another swim, John points out the high walls of a mansion. 'The owner of that house is the fella who invented the little plug that connects your Internet to the telephone socket.' Onwards we fly to Fenit.

MEENOGAHANE

Latitude: 52.44855
Longitude: -9.770585

Type: Bathing, swimming, coasteering.

When: High tide to low tide, though more to see and do at higher tides.

Access: Head north at the small crossroads at Ballynaskreena, onto the Meenogahane Pier Road.

Safety: No lifeguard but safe, secluded pier and bay. Care should be taken when walking or jumping from rocks.

John Edwards and Hannah Lloyd overlooking the rocky coastline.

ask John casually what distances he would be capable of covering at sea. 'Oh, about twenty kilometres or so.' Surfer, diver, lifeguard and open-sea swimmer, John is, you might say, at home in the water. But it wasn't always so. 'I remember once in my early teens we had a sea-based swim in Fenit, where I swam from the pier to the Tralee Bay slip. I saw a fish, and so got out and walked back.'

Neither of John's parents was a swimmer but he took to the pool as a young boy, swimming for the Kingdom Club in Tralee. It wasn't until the age of seventeen that he made the transition to sea swimming. His interest at that point shifted to surfing, but in Ireland surfing is more of a winter sport, beginning in September when the swells pick up and the hurricane season bites. The long break over the summer sees the surf season arrive again, but finds many surfers without 'match fitness'.

'I started going out with the Tralee Bay Swimming Club and I really took to it. I found myself addicted to it. When I finished work I needed to get out to Fenit. I was doing it to November, then doing the Christmas Day swim, then the surfing would kick in again. So I was in the ocean all the time.' The Tralee Bay Swimming Club has been here since the 1950s, with about eighty members currently. It has its own slip into safe, south-facing waters, protected from westerly or south-westerly swells. Buoys mark out 100m and 150m intervals.

John Edwards chats to an old friend in the sea.

Redeveloped bathing area at Fenit.

When the recession hit, John's delivery company was put out of business by larger competitors. 'I was free that summer and at a loose end so I offered to coach open-water swimming. I was scratching my head when they all went back to school, and I needed to find something to do. So I did a lot of hillwalking and climbing, kayaking and surfing, things that I'd been doing in my spare time for years.' John spent the next year and a half becoming an instructor in mountaineering, kayaking, rock climbing, swimming, surfing and coasteering.

At the same time, John got asked to do more and more coaching work, with both the Tralee Bay and the Kingdom Clubs. Both clubs now share the newly built facilities at Fenit. He also coaches the Triathlon club and trains swimmers on a one-to-one basis. Swimming and the sea have become his livelihood.

'Yesterday morning, I had a guy who wants to be able to swim from the Tralee Bay swimmers' slip to Fenit Beach, about 700m. That's his goal. Some people are training for the half-Ironman in Dublin, so there's the competitive side of things. But the type of swimming that I've grown to love the most is swimming from A to B, where I'm under no pressure. I get dropped to a place in a boat, my son will be in the kayak, and I'll just swim at my own pace. I'll stop and enjoy it as I go along.'

And Fenit is the heart of club swimming in Kerry. Everything here revolves around the sea and swimming. On Christmas day, Mike's Beach Hut Café opens to serve its summertime regulars. The beach opposite is flooded with more than 700 swimmers who are joined by thousands of onlookers, all to raise money for the local RNLI.

John speaks with passion about sea swimming and shares some sensible ideas. A lot of people bemoan the fact that so many kids rely on wetsuits for a swim but John believes that anything keeping kids in the sea is a positive. He's keen to encourage more kids to learn to swim.

'I see boys of eight, nine, ten years of age with armbands on. One hundred and twenty-seven people drown on average each year. We're an island nation, we're surrounded by sea. Everyone should learn to swim and learn to respect the ocean.'

FENIT

Latitude: 52.274356
Longitude: -9.873324

Type: Distance swimming, training, bathing.

When: High to low tide.

Access: Follow the R558 through Kilfenora to Fenit, follow the pathway south-west of the beach on foot.

Safety: Safe enclosed waters.

Clare 7

All sorts on sale outside Nolan's of Kilkee.

25 Pollock Holes

Picture this: on a hot summer's day in the 1970s, posters are plastered on every second window and noticeboard of Kilkee town, announcing that the great Italian divers – the Benzini Brothers – are to perform at 3 p.m. that very day. They are to appear at Newfoundout, a popular swimming area in the West End with diving boards offering jumps of up to 30ft. Word spreads quickly and soon the town is humming with the news. Kids in their Sunday best drag their parents down to the sea. Grannies and granddads treat themselves to ice creams and head for the large Romanesque steps. Holidaying nuns and priests indulge in the Sabbath day spectacle and join the gathering crowds.

At exactly 3 p.m., the great actor Richard Harris and a friend step forth from the changing room bollock naked, tread the boards, so to speak, and dive in. They swim out across the bay and don't stop till they reach Byrne's Cove. And that was the last Kilkee saw of the great Benzinis. Or at least that's the story that came to us third hand.

Scenes of the rocky landscape from the cliff walk above.

It was months later that I learned from Manuel Di Lucia, son of Italian immigrants but born and raised in Kilkee, and an old friend of Dickie, as he was known, that the story was a complete fabrication. It is true beyond doubt that Richard Harris spent his summers in Kilkee, when his family would make the journey from their home in Limerick to stay in the Georgian terraces of the upmarket West End. Here Harris regularly dived, posed and flirted at the Newfoundout diving boards, performed dangerous stunts at height, and would swim across the bay, a one-mile journey, to Byrne's Cove, then a men's nudist beach. We were also told that the Brontë sisters had stayed in the same house as Harris later stayed in (in fact, Charlotte Brontë honeymooned nearby); and that two wall murals of Che Guevara remember his 'visit' to the town (though he spent only a night in the Strand Hotel after a delayed stopover at Shannon Aiport). Kilkee, it appears, is a town where stories go to prosper.

Harris also swam at the nearby Pollock Holes, a beautiful Burren-esque reef which the tides cover over, leaving behind three deep pools of calm water that warm in the sun once the water recedes. The Pollock Holes are best at lower tides, when all three pools are accessible.

Children at play at the busy Pollock Hole 1.

Che Guevara makes his mark on the town walls.

Top: Peter Wallace and Brendan in Pollock Hole 1.

Facing page: Underwater action at Pollock Hole 1.

On the first day Michael and I arrive, it is already a couple of hours after low tide. A crowd of forty or so, made up mostly of young families, are gathered around Pool 1 and are leaping into its clear deep waters. We are joined for the day by our friend Peter Wallace, who is equally amazed by the beauty of these deep pools. While the diving boards at Newfoundout are still waiting to be replaced, the water depth at Pool 1 is perfect for me to get some much-needed diving practice. Everything is beginning to come together, except at the last moment – as Michael regularly points out – when my legs bend and part, and the whole thing comes asunder.

While Pool 1, nearest the café, was traditionally reserved for women only, it was in practice used by all. The adventurously named Pool 2 was a mixed bathing spot – very forward thinking – and Pool 3, further from the shoreline, was men only, and a nude bathing area at that.

I heard Pool 3 was not to be missed, so Michael and I return the next day at exactly the right tide time. It is much cooler and dark clouds loom. I am just about able to coax Michael in, although he is full of the joys of life on leaving the water, a good ten minutes after I do, despite the fact that it is by then lashing down on our heads. As we walk back across the rocks in heavy rain, a father and three children continue to explore Pool 2 while the mother and youngest child struggle back alongside us over increasingly slippery rocks.

POLLOCK HOLES

Latitude: 52.682923
Longitude: -9.665858

Type: Bathing, snorkelling.

When: After high tide.

Access: Follow the coast road west from Kilkee town, heading for the Diamond Rock Café.

Safety: No lifeguard.

26 Kerin's Hole

'Is that John Creedon, the Wild Atlantic Way fellow?' asks a passer-by as we head for Kerin's Hole. We're in the company of Johnny St John who is a dead ringer for Creedon. He's also the local guide for our swim at Kerin's Hole, a small deep pool beneath the cliffs by White Strand. He grew up and has lived his life in the nearby town of Miltown Malbay and spends his summers living on the Strand.

I must warn you: this is a feel-good story. And Johnny tells it with the help of his wife, Anne, as well as their friends Eileen and Pauline. Together with Michael and Peter, we're huddled around pre-swim cups of tea in Johnny's mobile home.

'We'd be down at ten or eleven in the morning, leave our gear with the lifeguard, swim across the bay to Kerin's Hole, and stay out till 6 p.m.,' says Johnny, remembering his childhood days. But until recently, access to Kerin's Hole was precarious. 'It fell into ruin over the years, the steps just fell away. And the ladder broke and fell away too. So after Christmas in 2012, a few of us got together to talk about what we might do.'

Opening the new cliff access to Kerin's Hole in summer 2013.

By January, two local groups – Save the White Strand (headed by Johnny) and Miltown Malbay Tidy Towns – were already at work. Within six months Kerin's Hole had been restored to its former glory, ready for the June bank holiday and the summer heatwave of 2013. 'The thing about it was, everyone in the town would have fantastic memories of that place. It was all the older generation that chipped in,' says Pauline.

To begin the fundraising, they sold steps for €100 a pop, but they very quickly sold out. 'We were asking ourselves, how many steps can we make, how long is the ladder going to be?' A plaque at the top of the cliff steps commemorates all those involved in the work, and three individual plaques were bought at €500 in memory of lost loved ones. 'We raised €17,000,' says Pauline, 'and that was without begging. Nobody begged.'

They also raised money by organising a water-themed celebrity couples night out. 'There were a lot of David Hasselhoffs,' says Eileen. 'Two neighbouring farmers, Junior Carroll and Tommy Vaughan, men in their fifties and sixties, won the competition. They sold lines of tickets at every mart for weeks in advance of the night, but they handed over their trophy to the moral victors – Father Seany, who had paired up with the sacristan, Ann. They came together dressed as an old couple.' It was Father Seany who later

Mucking around in the pool at full tide.

Brendan in off the rocks.

Lads at play all day in their wetsuits.

Anne, Pauline and Eileen.

blessed Kerin's Hole in front of a crowd of hundreds, and Ann the sacristan who cut the ribbon. 'We have a lovely priest in Father Seany,' adds Pauline.

Marine engineer Louis Keating agreed to take on the reconstruction of Kerin's Hole. An enormous digger came from the Belfast docks with a long-reaching arm that scaled over the cliff edge to bore holes for the steps. Both Louis and his foremen worked gratis and the materials were provided at cost. 'The money wouldn't have been anywhere near enough had we paid the actual cost,' admits Johnny.

The name behind the swimming spot remains a mystery. Johnny did some research into it at the time of the redevelopment but nobody provided a conclusive answer. 'We were in Kerin's Hole last week,' says Johnny, 'about four or five of us, and there were a couple of strangers there, too. One of them asked me how Kerin's Hole got its name, and I said, "Sure didn't yer man of the Kerins get shot at the top of the cliff and he fell to his death." About twenty minutes later I could hear the two of them behind us, talking, "He did, he got shot on this cliff and fell off."' And so another story is born. The Ordnance Survey map records Kerin's Point, though no name hangs over the swimming spot.

But Pauline has her own theory: 'Wasn't it that the parish was blessed so that nobody would ever be killed with lightning – that was in it. And it was Father Kerin that blessed it. That's why I've no fear of lightning when I'm swimming at Kerin's.' We wouldn't have gotten wind of Kerin's Hole but for a few locals who emailed us with proud stories of its restoration. One of them, Patricia Fitzpatrick, kindly offered us a place to stay. Little did we know she was calling around, looking for one of the last B&B beds in town, and at her own expense. And the following night, Eileen and her husband Francis cook us a pot roast to remember.

We are staying above O'Loughlin's Bar. Peadar, the landlord, remembers his friend Holly diving from the top of the cliffs into Kerin's Hole below. It doesn't seem possible now given the distance from the cliff edge to the pool, but it's likely that the cliffs have been washed away in the meantime. Indeed, Peadar passed the spot recently and didn't recognise it, so much of the cliffs have been eroded in the storms of recent winters.

Kerin's Hole lives up to our expectations – a deep natural pool that's good for a swim a couple of hours either side of high tide, and good for a few dives too. Johnny's daughter Ava and some of her friends join us for the swim, beginning a whole new generation of good memories. Then it's back to Johnny's mobile home for more tea and biscuits, and on to Cleary's Pub, aka Blonde's, where all three generations of fair-haired Cleary women are serving at the bar while the session roars.

KERIN'S HOLE

Latitude: 52.867466
Longitude: -9.433005

Type: Bathing.

When: Ideal an hour or two either side of high tide.

Access: Turn off the N67 at Fintra More for White Strand. Kerin's Hole is situated along the cliff walk on the right-hand side of the beach.

Safety: Nearby White Strand is a sheltered blue-flag beach. Kerin's Hole is not lifeguarded.

27 Clahane

Impending rain at Clahane.

On the road to Clahane we pass Donald Trump's golf course at Doonbeg, with three flags flying: Ireland's, America's and his own flag, black, very much like that of a pirate. The radio is telling us that it's 400 days to the US presidential election. We imagine a world with Donald Trump as its leader: more golf, fewer Mexicans; more cut-throat business, fewer wind turbines; and misshapen comb-overs for all. His inheritance to the local swimming community has been an attempt to block a right of way to swimmers and surfers that has existed at Doonbeg since time immemorial.

Kids are warring over great piles of seaweed when we arrive, 'Get away from that seaweed, it's ours,' they cry. They have woven Rambo-style bandanas made from kelp around their foreheads – the dark green camouflage colouring is perfect – and they lash the air with whips of thick weed. Afterwards, they pose for photos with their parents.

Nearly all of the kids are in wetsuits. I am delighted to see it, if only because it makes me feel a bit hardier than I really am, even if I'm out of the water after fifteen minutes and they stay in for the next two hours. It was the same at the Pollock Holes where one father proudly told us how his two kids, a boy and girl of perhaps ten and twelve, were the only two swimming without suits. 'I never had a suit when I was a young fella,' he said as if to imply, 'it's a bloody disgrace.' His poor kids.

'LEEGGS!' shouts Michael as I dive in from the height of a foot. The tide is fully in and the kids line up to dive beside the single steel ladder. It doesn't stop us from diving alongside them as Michael continues the lesson. Michael's body is straight as an arrow as it enters the water. Mine is still good for the first part of the dive and then, as ever, the legs part, the knees bend and I look like a tall, gangly child being flung into the sea by his feckless father.

Mammies take their eye off the action but Michael (bottom left) with his camera at the ready.

All sorts of things can go wrong with a dive. If you jump in feet first but forget to bring your feet together, the water is going to rush up between your legs to meet you where it hurts. If you dive in head first but forget to punch the water with your outstretched arms, you're going to headbutt the stuff, which won't hurt the water but may leave you with a slap mark on your forehead.

Once, at the Forty Foot, I was looking forward to diving in so much that I forgot to close my eyes. I simply watched the water as it rushed towards my face. As soon as my eyes made contact with the water my vision flashed white, then suddenly turned pitch black. I shut my eyes and kept them squeezed closed. It felt like a long time coming up for air and I wondered what I'd see, or if I'd see, when I surfaced. A wave of relief, or perhaps just a wave, washed over me when I opened them again. We've all had our little scares with the sea.

CLAHANE

Latitude: 52.932348
Longitude: -9.420784

Type: Bathing.

When: Better at higher tides.

Access: At Lahinch, turn off the N67 towards Liscannor on the R478. After passing through Liscannor, turn left for Clahane, and left again onto the coast road.

Safety: No lifeguard. Beware of submerged rocks.

I had been in Clahane last summer – 'the good summer' – in beautiful sunshine, and at lower tide, though still swimmable. A child of eight or so was standing by the steps and staring at a lone jellyfish impeding his entry, and a team of adults at hand were monitoring its movements. While we are continually being told that we should have travelled the coastline last summer, we are delighted to find noticeably fewer jellyfish this year. Today's swim at Clahane is no exception. The deep blue waters are jellyfish free; the payoff is having to dry ourselves off as the rain comes down on top of us again.

Galway 8

Inis Mór

28 Blackrock

I collect Michael from North Great George's Street in Dublin's north inner city a little earlier than usual. We're on the road again, driving from coast to coast, city to city, hoping to get to Galway's Blackrock in time for high-tide diving. We are listening to a rare thing on the radio – a Dub speaking faster than a Corkonian. Dave Fanning has taken over from Brendan O'Connor on RTÉ Radio 1; we're now into the month of August. We make Salthill in under three hours, including a caffeine-and-scone stop.

The swimming spots that belong to cities by the sea are incredibly special. They have the critical mass of population to ensure that you'll always meet a fellow dipper, no matter the time, no matter the weather. Well, almost.

And the vast majority of swimmers who frequent these spots, such as the Forty Foot, Guillamene and Blackrock, are social swimmers, swimming or plunging for early-morning refreshment to set themselves up for the day.

Busy day at Blackrock.

Winter swimmers might stay in for as little as five seconds, but the overall experience might take up to an hour – pre-swim banter and post-swim tea, or maybe something stronger. There is no other pastime that sees people from such diverse age ranges or social backgrounds commune and form friendships. With no other social act does one person confer on the other such immediate respect or give them the time of day without question, simply because they're about to share the sea together. (The possible exception to both of these statements being the institution of the Irish pub.) Regular swimmers at all of these spots invariably use the word 'camaraderie'.

Swimmers have been coming to Salthill and Blackrock for centuries. The increasing popularity of seaweed baths and 'taking the waters' for health throughout the nineteenth century confirmed Salthill as a seaside resort. In 1885 a rickety old board attached to a large A-frame stretched out into the

Back flip from the top platform.

sea from Blackrock – it was the area's first diving platform. It was replaced in the early twentieth century by a more ambitious structure built from steel and wood that lasted into the 1940s but became dangerous and decrepit. In 1954, a diving platform, designed by a local engineer, built by a local construction company and blessed by the local priest, was opened – to men only, of course. Bishops patrolled the area ensuring that the men stayed in Salthill and the ladies stuck to the nearby Ladies' Beach, though the women eventually joined the men at Blackrock in the 1970s.

Among the daily swimmers out in force today are the fickle summer dippers and divers like myself and Michael. We knock around with some teenagers who are somersaulting from the top platform, dodging the three or four compass jellyfish drifting below. An accomplished show-off with long flowing hair takes running, bouncing, head-first leaps from the top board, reeling back to touch his feet in mid-air. Oohs and ahhs rise from the onlookers.

I approach another diver, Mike Doyle, who is a little more measured in his form. He is diving head-first with an elegant rigidity from the top platform. Alongside him is his daughter, Isabel, who at the tender age of seven is jumping feet-first from the highest platform for her very first time. That's a 24ft drop for a girl of little more than 4ft tall.

Mike grew up in Galway but is now living in Rathgar in Dublin. I ask him if he remembers his first time jumping from the top. 'I do, in fact, though I stood up there for a good two hours before jumping in,' he admits. 'I'm not sure if it's still the same but we used to keep diving until the tide dropped down to the third metal step below the diving tower. After that you're hitting sand, and that's when you need to jump out further.'

And as the tide hits the third step, just as Mike remembered, the lifeguards pull the plug on our fun, closing the gates to the top platforms and blocking entry to the lower diving ledges. But there are plenty of hours of swimming left in the day as hordes of people continue to arrive in the sun and file in via steps to the sea.

BLACKROCK

Latitude: 53.256195
Longitude: -9.092207

Type: Bathing, diving, distance swimming.

When: Swimming at high to low tide, diving at higher tides only.

Access: From Galway city, head west along the R336. Stick to the coast and you won't miss it.

Safety: Lifeguards on duty. Check depths before diving. Relatively sheltered waters for swimming.

Mike Doyle executes expert dives from the top platform.

We are drinking pints in the American Bar and Michael must have a look on his face or a twinkle in his eye, because he draws the attention of a sage old man by the bar, who had been keeping to himself and soaking up the music. He says to Michael, 'I think you need a peeysh of adviysh.' 'Do I indeed?' says Michael, ready for an earful. And the enlightened one offers forth his pearl: 'You only need five things in life: ceol, ól, feoil, the dole and yer rock 'n' roll.'

Earlier in the day, Michael and I are met off the boat by Jackie Roantree, an old friend of Michael's who has lived on Inis Mór for the past twenty-four years. Still a blow-in of course, and a jackeen from Dublin's North Strand at that, but she is very much recognised on the island as she drives us from one spot to another – the Pier House for lunch and a pint, Trá Mór for a swim and some yoga, back to her home on 'the airport road' that overlooks

Jackie Roantree practising yoga on the beach.

both the beach and the grave of her late husband, Sean Roantree, a sailor who captained the ferry from Rossaveel to Kilronan. Then we head back to the pier at Kilronan for a high-tide swim with the kids, both locals and holidaymakers. Later we push on to the American Bar, then Watty's, for live music, dancing and a feed of pints.

The island is packed with great places to swim, including Trá na bhFrancach and Kilmurvey. We don't make it to the famous Poll na bPéist (Worm Hole), where the spring high tide is bringing water in over the shelf of rock, making it too dangerous to enter. Trá Mór is our swimming highlight; it's a little off the beaten track, so if you manage to make it out by foot, bike or taxi, you'll probably be the only person on the beach, even on a hot summer day in midseason, with the white sand and cool, turquoise waters all to yourself.

But we manage to knock a week's worth of craic out of a one-night stay. Much is unlearned in the course of a night's drinking, but being on an island in a Gaeltacht region that has attracted great scholars like ourselves for centuries, we manage to fill that void with some new terminology as

Trá Mór.

Jackie and Michael acting up.

Swimmers in for an evening dip at the pier in Kilronan.

well as the aforementioned piece of local wisdom, which we're putting to good use.

Sonta Salach: A shady stretch of sea, a few filthy kilometres between Inis Oírr and Inis Meáin. A Japanese gent living on Inis Oírr for the past ten years or so, a quiet fellow we're told, swam it with a local fisherman at his side; no big promos or bragging. Currents and swell galore. Literally, 'the dirty sound'.

CIT: Craggy Island Tours, a caravan-based tourist office, parked outside of Tí Joe Watty. Full to the rafters with auld tat and junk. Doors nail-gunned shut. It was the caravan – from the outside, at least – in which Ted and Dougal spent the night with Father Noel Furlong and the St Luke's Youth Group. 'Some of us overdid it down the old local last night! Gerry Fields knows who I'm talking about!' But the caravan in which they'd actually filmed was much larger. 'These are small, but the ones out there are far away.'

Little Tents: A new band bangin' out the tunes in the American Bar. Formed with the help of the Edge and Bono. But don't hold it against them … Bono does be skinny-dipping down by the Vico betimes.

Peggy's Hole: Not a place where you get yer rock 'n' roll; rather, a swimming spot on Inis Oírr where you might take the waters.

Roadjeen: A small road. 'Not a bohareen, a roadjeen. I'm from the island, I think I'd know.'

Coladh Snámh: What you might say to someone as an ironic twist on 'coladh sámh' before they go for a swim. And what a lesser Gaeilgeoir might look down at you for saying, in the belief that you've made a basic linguistic error.

The Vassindoolins: A German settler, common on the west coast of Ireland, who learned to play trad ceol in the county Clare. 'Jah, I vass in Doolin.'

INIS MÓR

Latitude: 53.104187
Longitude: -9.643378

Type: Variety of spots listed.

When: Beaches and pier at all tides. Poll na bPéist at higher tides, depending on the moon cycle.

Access: Ferry from Doolin or Rossaveel, or flights from Connemara airport.

Safety: Poll na bPéist is frequently unsafe; caution and local advice recommended.

Wild flowers in the dunes above Trá Mór.

30 Errisbeg Peninsula

As the journey progresses, a lyric from The Police keeps revolving in my head, and as we walk Gurteen Beach I sing aloud: 'Giant steps are what you take, walking on the moon.' Pressing feet into soft white sand, passing boulders bearded with lichen and stepping through warm boggy puddles, I can't help but feel I'm traversing an alien landscape. I manage to spot the sole mushroom growing on this peninsula, near shrivelled, with a slice taken out of it. It looks more like a mushroom that's been rotting away at the back of a fridge than one alive. We walk all four beaches, dip our toes in the waters of all four too, but we only swim at one: the beach with no name. It is only as I show Michael the three beaches on the map that we notice it – a sliver of beach, a cove within a bay.

The longer Gurteen Beach on the southern side is backed by the shorter dog's-leg beach on the northern side. Follow either to its western end where the peninsula explodes into a stunning headland. There are two more beaches here that go unmentioned in most guides of the area.

The larger of the two, facing due south, has the most extraordinary tomb-like stone with a natural wreath of wild flowers growing on top. We arrive at the smallest beach last. We thought we'd be alone but three ladies of middle age are just drying off from their swim. They are reading and meditating, facing the falling sun. The water is cool and clear, and deepens quickly. We're out of our depth within 20 metres, though the white sand, dotted with seaweed, is still visible below.

The variety of terrain on this one small headland rewards a couple of hours' walk, though you might go barefoot or bring your wellies, even in dry weather. The swallows flit from their burrowed dwellings in the walls of the dunes. They compete for real estate with the numerous hares that dash quickly out of sight.

We decide to give the beach a name, and decide also to be unoriginal in our choice. The influence of the Catholic Church seems to have played an integral part in the naming (and the policing) of Irish bathing spots. There are devil's creeks, caves and holes in some of the rockier locations. There

Looking back onto Gurteen.

Trá na Triúr Ban.

A picturesque scene on the road to Ballyconneely.

Tomb-like rock with natural wreath growing on top.

are numerous nuns' beaches, coves and islands spread about the country; it seems that nuns loved nothing other than a good dip after a long day at prayer. The separation of women and men in public life has led to numerous ladies' beaches too, the alternative to the once-numerous male nude bathing areas. In this instance, I presume, the ladies bathing here have not been shooed off Dog's Bay or Gurteen Beach, but have come of their own good wisdom. So we dub it Trá na Triúr Ban. As the evening deepens and we walk from Dog's Bay back to Gurteen, a swallow executes fly-bys and circles around us; has it heard from the gulls that humans are easy pickings? During the week, another swimmer makes the news after being attacked at Fenit, with skin broken.

When we arrive back to the car, the tide is in and I realise I have been here before, at the age of twelve or thereabouts, staying in a family friend's holiday home for a couple of weeks. A banana boat ride stands out in my mind. There is no banana boat on offer now. Perhaps claims against the company for whiplash put an end to it. But the bay still has its share of small motor boats, pulling waterskiers along at a fair old clip.

Despite our summer journey, we get jealous easily. We envy the families staying in the mobile homes just above Gurteen. Imagine their long day on the beach, followed by a shower, and a first beer before lighting the barbeque out on the deck. Yes, mobile home decking. The Celtic Tiger was good for something.

Gurteen as the tide recedes.

ERRISBEG PENINSULA

Latitude: 53.3774
Longitude: -9.970994

Type: Bathing, distance swimming.

When: High to low tide.

Access: On the R341 between Roundstone and Ballyconneely.

Safety: All four beaches set in sheltered, calm and clear waters.

(31) Glassilaun

Imagine that you're locked in a dark room for days on end and you don't know what time of day or night it is. Now imagine you've just been let out of the room and you see the sun fixed just above the horizon. What are the signs by which you'd know it was morning and not evening, or vice versa? Or would you know at all? I put that question to Michael on the road from Letterfrack to Glassilaun.

'The cold,' says Michael. 'The dew,' I say. And we wonder aloud together at all the ways by which you could tell it was morning. The breaking mist, the wakening flowers. On this morning, there is a peculiar class of light, with a paleness to it despite the rising sun.

On the gently sloping road towards Glassilaun Beach I lash on the handbrake. Have you ever seen a sleeping cow? I hadn't, and I'm surprised by the odd turn of its neck, slung back over its shoulder like a swan's. Here I am, a Dub let loose in the wilds of Galway, taking photos of sleeping cattle. It seems impossible now that my life could get any better.

We walk the beach to get the measure of it. Glassilaun is a severely horseshoed bay, with rocky outcrops on either side to explore, ideal for snorkellers and divers. Dead jellyfish are thick on the shoreline, being collected by the rising tide, but the eastern end of the beach appears to be clear so we enter the water here. The fish are still sleeping, though crabs scuttle by on the sand below.

This is the setting for the west of Ireland's largest scuba and diving centre. We dropped in to meet Breffni Gray who runs Scubadive West with his brother Cillian. Breffni is preparing to take a group snorkelling from their own private slipway that leads onto a shallow reef, then further around to Killary Fjord. 'You get people who haven't really spent time in the sea,' says Breffni, 'coming from all over Ireland, Germany and France, from landlocked countries and industrial cities. This blows their mind. The North Atlantic Drift creates a nutrient-rich environment along the whole of the west. People who've never worn a mask before put one on for the first time, and straight away, in waist-deep water, there's small crabs and plaice, and cuttlefish squirting ink. It's amazing, particularly at this time of year.'

Breffni remembers scouting around the west of Ireland, looking for a new location to expand the business which his father Shane had started in Dalkey in the mid-1970s. The estate agent was keen to show them around the building, but Breffni and his dad were suited and booted to dive. 'It was on a beautiful day like this one. There were thornback ray and cuttlefish flying around – an amazing variety of life that you wouldn't see on the east coast. We came out of the water with the scuba gear still on and gave the agent the thumbs up. We hadn't even looked at the house.'

Top: Glassilaun Beach. Middle: Cow awakens.
Below: 'There's a certain slant of light.' On the road into Glassilaun.

Glassilaun Beach is slightly more exposed to the swell on a choppy day, and signs in the car park suggest which side of the beach to swim, depending on wind directions, but Breffni confirms that you'll see a similar variety of life. 'Where you have a big expanse of sand, you won't get as much in the way of pollock – they're looking for camouflage while they're hunting – and small fish prefer the shelter of rocks, but the edges on either side of the beach provide good snorkelling and diving.'

Breffni takes more advanced divers to the islands off the coast of Mayo where they had also considered setting up business – Inishturk and Clare Island. The latter is our next port of call.

Rotting boat and lobster pots.

GLASSILAUN

Latitude: 53.614919
Longitude: -9.877803

Type: Bathing, swimming, snorkelling.

When: High to low tide.

Access: Set on the Connemara Loop, search for Scubadive West.

Safety: No lifeguard but safe and sheltered.

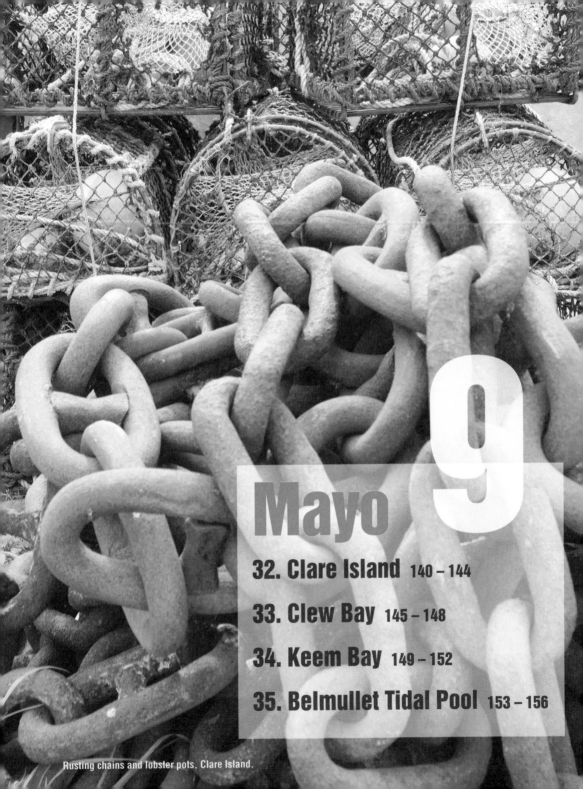

Mayo

9

Rusting chains and lobster pots, Clare Island.

32 Clare Island

'Did you hear the one about the headmistress?' a young boy is asking a girl of the same age, the pair of them no more than nine or ten. They are loafing around on the old stone pier that splits the beach. 'They were on a school tour and she took him into her tent and she raped him!' The wind is blowing their conversation across to day trippers unloading from the boat, pretending not to hear. 'Do gays and lesbians have sex with each other?' she asks him. 'Do you like Gae-lic,' he asks, 'Gay lick?' *Merciful hour*, I think, as I lean in to catch another snippet.

The two larger piers where the ferries dock are deep and good for jumping, though they're busy with the trade of the island's fishing industry. The beach beside them is beautiful though unextraordinary. We are after a third place, the holy grail of swimming spots, known simply as 'The Cove'.

Michael and I have The Cove marked with an X on a tourist map, yet we lose our concentration under the hot sun and set off on the wrong road from the get-go, south-west towards the post office. We ask a passer-by who kindly sends us back the way we came. This time we head north-west towards Clare Island Lighthouse, situated on the most northerly tip of the island.

The Cove with beautiful, deep, crystal clear water.

The Cove.

There is a bit of toing and froing and second-guessing ourselves. We arrive at where we think the turn-off should be. The map is telling us we're at the right crossroads. However, the GPS on our phones, when it's working, is telling us there is no path here. Google Maps gives no sign of it. The day is white hot and the sun is belting down on us. I begin to hallucinate. An ancient bearded mystic with the head of a goat on a donkey's frame appears on the road, ready to lead us to the Promised Land. First at a distance, suddenly near us, and suddenly gone.

And then a taxi-bus passes. We hail it and ask its driver how we might get to The Cove. 'You're nearly there,' she says, 'just down there towards the house.' And she points to a track that doesn't exist. 'When you reach the wall turn left and you'll see the path.'

We do as she says, walking towards a lone farmhouse with the words 'Private Property' spray-painted on its wall. But instead of riling up the

Dolphins join our boat ride back to the mainland.

farmer, we make a ninety-degree left turn and find ourselves on a submerged mud track, sloppy and wet even on this arid afternoon. It leads down to a gap in the fields, where a stream running through beds of fern opens into a narrow creek, and a vision of paradise.

The sun cuts through the deep water, lighting up The Cove, clarifying the detail of the seabed – in parts sandy, weedy and stony. We dive from the rocks just above the waterline, though jumping from the pier head looks possible at higher tides. A lone fishing boat is tied up in The Cove and a quad bike is parked nearby with containers to carry lobster, mackerel or pollock back up the steep, muddy track. We meet a woman on her lunch break. She works at the lighthouse and is waiting for a friend to join her for a swim. The Cove was developed as a pier where boats could drop off supplies for the lighthouse, she tells us, before lying out in the sun to fall asleep.

Michael showing good form.

Wild conversation carries on the wind from the old pier, Clare Island Beach.

On our way back up the hill we are passed by a broad form, decked in layers of jumpers, towels and cloaks; footed in clogs and goggled at the eyes; topped off with a bubbled swim cap.

Michael is about 50 metres ahead of me and when I catch him up he says, 'I hope you got a picture of that.' 'Oh Jesus,' I think, 'I absolutely should have.' My amateur photographer's instinct has failed me. But then I reason, 'What was I supposed to say to her, "Sorry, missus, you look absolutely bananas, do you mind if I take a photo?"' 'Fair enough,' agrees Michael, 'Fair enough.'

Field? Bog? Forest? Perhaps all three. On the road to The Cove.

CLARE ISLAND

Latitude: 53.821118
Longitude: -9.970459

Type: Bathing.

When: High to low tide.

Access: Take the road to the lighthouse, at Ballytoohy More turn right off the main road, heading north-east across the muddy track.

Safety: No lifeguard, calm water in the small pier. lifeguard.

33 Clew Bay

You won't go hungry at the Gannon household. The eggs we have with breakfast are from the chicken coop across the road. There is a meat feast of a breakfast to go with them, served with brown bread and infinite hot drops of tae. Later, of the thirty or so mackerel we catch over a fifteen-minute period on the near side of Inishoo, seven or eight are gutted and fried within ten minutes of our arrival ashore by Ger's mother in her house next door. They are served alongside half a dozen fresh oysters from his brother's shellfish farm. A homemade apple tart is dropped in by his sister Caroline for dessert, along with a small jug of cream. 'I didn't put any rhubarb in,' she says. 'I know Alan prefers it without.' When we finally leave in the late afternoon, it is with a box of oysters in tow, covered in seaweed to keep them cool.

We were invited to Ger's home in Roslaher on the pretext of going for a swim. I was put in touch with Ger in a very Irish way – he is a friend's brother's wife's brother-in-law. And he's mad for the sea.

'If you're looking for a swim in Clew Bay,' Ger says, 'there are too many places to list off.' But among the long list are Old Head Beach and Leckanvey on the south side of the bay and Mallaranny Beach on the north. To add to that, Clew Bay is pocked with islands. 'They say there are 365 in all, one for every day of the year, but in reality there are only about fifty-odd that you could really call an island.'

With Deirdre, Ger and their four kids all geared up for a swim, myself and Michael set off for Inishoo Island in their 21-footer, *The Golden Girl*. We pass Inishturk Beg and Ger tells us a Celtic Tiger tale. The 63-acre island was bought in 2003 by Irish-Egyptian businessman Nadim Sadek after a bidding war with ex-Boyzone singer Ronan Keating. Sadek was rumoured to have invested between €9 million and €20 million in the island, building five houses, roads, a sewerage system, a jetty, an all-weather sports field, a helipad and a grass-roofed, solar-heated swimming pool (on an island!). Sadek branded a range of luxury goods – whiskey, perfume, jewellery, cosmetics – in the island's name, but ten years after its purchase, Inishturk

Beg was sold by receivers to an anonymous UK investor for just under €3 million.

Rather than going for a swim first, and then fishing with the shivers after, we decide to drop a few lines. We stop the boat in the wake of Inishoo and unspool two lines of orange twine with seven feathered hooks. Ger drops the first, and as he hands it to me asks if there is something biting. It hasn't been in the water fifteen seconds when I pull it up rattling with mackerel. Seconds later and he is already taking in the second line; it's loaded like the first. As soon as the fish are unhooked and bucketed, we drop the lines again. Another fifteen seconds in the water and again we have seven mackerel apiece, two full lines. We can't see the shoal below but we are clearly dropping the feathers on their heads.

Ger is curious about Michael's city-centre roots – born in the Rotunda and living off Parnell Street twenty years and more. 'I don't know if this is a mad question,' asks Ger, 'but are there kids still growing up and spending their childhood in the city centre?' There are pros as well as cons to growing up in an urban environment, but Michael and I are continually wondering at the benefits of a childhood in the countryside, or more particularly, a childhood by the sea. There are great freedoms and a wider range of experiences to be had. Ger's youngest handles the mackerel with ease.

We set down the anchor on Inishoo, intending to swim in the lee of the island. But first a little exploration. Ger sometimes pitches a tent here and camps for the night. They think the island may be owned by Germans, though there is no house on it, no building at all, nor any features other than

View from Inishoo.

Donald Trump impressions with a knot of sheep's wool.

the natural. We climb to the top of the cliff and find a couple of mushrooms growing at the very edge. A clump of knotted sheep's wool lies on the grass so we take it in turns to do our best Donald Trump impression.

Back at the boat we delay the swim again, deciding to go nearer to the house, all the closer to the post-swim showers. But rather than swim, we take out 'le tube' and the kids take turns being whizzed around by the boat, holding on for dear life. Then Michael says it's my turn and raises some applause to get the big eejit to disrobe. In I go. And no sooner am I back in the boat than Michael is diving in off the edge of the boat, ready for his turn on the rubber tube. He stays in for a swim to add some validity to our day trip.

Back at the house I tell the Gannons that the Mac Evillys are originally from Mayo. Ger remembers an old school friend, Joe McEvilly, who had some

sage advice about the supping of two or three pints on a Monday evening after a heavy weekend. 'When you're at the top of a ladder, you don't jump off it; you come down slowly.' Another philosopher in the family.

On leaving, I try to convey my thanks to Deirdre and Ger. As with so many of our meetings on the road, I go away telling myself we really didn't deserve it. But we are thanked for having come in the first place, for giving them the excuse to get out on the sea for the day.

CLEW BAY

Latitude: 53.856789
Longitude: -9.668355

Type: Bathing, distance swimming.

When: High to low tide.

Access: N59 for numerous access points to the bay.

Safety: Look up safety information noticeboards at each individual beach/swimming spot.

Right: Mackerel are easy pickings in the bay.
Below: View over the cliff edge on Inishoo.

34 Keem Bay

Through illness and exhaustion, Michael and I miss Keem Bay the first time around. So it is mid-September and my last swim of the 'summer' when I return to Keem, at the tip of Achill Island, with my girlfriend Hannah, my sister Aoife and my parents. The Indian summer I had got wind of in late August never materialised, but the weather gods are working in our favour. The rain is pouring down on a cool east coast while we travel westward under skies that are opening in all the right places, with the midges making up for lost time.

The last of the montbretia is in bloom, the distinctive orange flowers mirrored in the changing colours of the leaves. The sun casts a shallow light over the landscape, pouring into mountain valleys.

Aoife and Hannah discover wild mint in the hedgerows of a byway and sample tart blackberries while I run back along the main road to take pictures. We pull in on a particularly bumpy stretch between Newport and Mallaranny. There is a road sign with a valuable double meaning, relevant to our swimming odyssey, that I want to capture on camera. Michael and I had zoomed past it on previous journeys in chains of traffic too long and fast to stop. This is our last chance. Hannah spots it on the road: '*Claonas Ceilte*: Hidden Dip.'

We arrive at Keem Bay to find a significant triangle of sand has been recently washed away by the outflowing stream, leaving behind a wide, stony delta. Strange stacks of sand are left sitting on large rocks as the earth-brown river merges with the azure-green sea.

Of the five people in the car, a swim for my mam is never in question. She hasn't been spotted in Irish waters in fifteen years or more. Dad comes for the journey but bows out too, and Hannah has conveniently left her bathing suit in the other car. The only other reliable swimmer in my family, the eldest sibling of five, Aoife, joins me for a dip.

Not since Guillamene in June have I swum in such cold water, and not since Clare Island have I swum in such clear water. This, of course, makes perfect sense, given that Clare Island can be seen from Keem Bay – only

20km in the distance. The water reveals greens of every hue, stretching to the tropical. We're not the only swimmers. Two other ladies who had shaken the beach with their shrieks on entry manage to lounge in the cold waters for nearly half an hour. We had followed them into the water and are well dry by the time they emerge.

Just behind the beach, a storyboard memorial documents Keem Bay's historic fishing industry. Keem was once home to Achill Island's basking shark fishery, one of four in Ireland, operating in a boom-to-bust industry from the 1940s through to the 1980s. Fishermen used traditional canvas-covered currachs (still seen on the beach today) and were directed by spotters situated on the cliffs above. They helped the boatmen trap sharks in enormous dragnets, sometimes aided with the use of harpoons.

View of Keem Bay from above.

Brendan and Aoife in for a leisurely paddle.

The recorded catch of basking shark in 1947 was just six. This rose rapidly in 1952 with a catch of 1,808, declining to figures in the low hundreds caught each year through the late 1950s, and down to double figures through the next two decades. At least 10,000 are thought to have been landed in the Achill Island fishery alone during those years. To put those figures in context, the current world population of basking shark is thought to be fewer than 10,000.

Records of shark fishing in the area date back to the late 1700s. They were fished for their oil, which was burned in the street lamps of Dublin, Belfast and Cork, as well as in the oil lamps of the more salubrious homes of these cities – ideal for this purpose as it is odourless when burned. It was also used in the lubrication of machinery and was applied to sprains and painful joints. The carcasses were originally driven to Castlebar to be turned into fish meal, though this became financially unviable in the mid-1950s, much to the relief of local communities along the route which had had to put up with the stench of the meat slopping onto the road as the trucks passed. Under EU and UK regulation, basking sharks are no longer fished in European waters.

Clew Bay and Achill Island are still home to numerous fisheries, including salmon, sea trout, oysters, mussels, abalone and sea urchins. The presence of so much fish farming is a good sign for swimmers as it indicates very clean waters.

Remains of the old fishing industry.

KEEM BAY

Latitude: 53.96773
Longitude: -10.192931

Type: Bathing.

When: High to low tide.

Access: Take the R319 heading west to the end of the road.

Safety: Rip current sometimes present. Blue-flag beach with lifeguard.

35 Belmullet Tidal Pool

We travel northward to Belmullet, catch Mayo's drubbing of Donegal in the All-Ireland quarter-final at the Broadhaven Bay Hotel, then bed down on the Shore Road overlooking Blacksod Bay. We have a date at ten o'clock the following morning. We're skipping Mass and off for a swim at the Belmullet tidal pool.

The Shore Road has always been a popular swimming spot in the town of Belmullet. 'Back in the 1950s and 1960s it was men only who swam at the Shore Road,' says Eva Reilly, who was the Water Safety Officer for Belmullet during the 1980s. 'We started swimming there in the mid-1960s. The parish priest, Archdeacon Feeney, complained about us from the altar, but we were brazen and chose to ignore him. He was in his seventies then and used to swim there himself. We made life difficult for him.'

Eva and her friends would swim from the slipway, which led out to a rock about 30m from the shoreline. It was considered a rite of passage for following generations of young swimmers to make it to the rock and dive off at high tide. 'We spent our summers at the slip,' says Eva, 'let away in the morning, only returning for a meal in the evening.'

Eva Reilly (left) enjoys the swim despite the weather.

It is directly to the left of this rock that the tidal pool is set. Its story begins with one family's holiday to Sweden in the early 1980s. Belmullet was in need of an indoor swimming pool, but in the prevailing economy it was a non-runner. However, Ann Maguire, a local swimmer on the Shore Road, spotted a tidal pool on her Swedish holiday and took notes. She believed something similar could be installed in Belmullet. On her return, with the help of local engineer Paddy McManamon, they drew up plans for the pool.

Ann McGuire was one of five women, along with Eva Reilly, who were part of the Belmullet Swimming Club. Like the swimmers at Kerin's Hole, they raised money to get their project off the ground, and in 1984 the pool was built.

The tidal pool on a fine September evening.

The design of the pool is not without its flaws. The walls were built too high, preventing daily tides from refilling the pool. It relies on bimonthly spring tides to refill it. During the summer months, the water can become stagnant and unsafe to swim in. To prevent this, the fire brigade are called in (but only on a Wednesday, their training day) to release water through the pool's valves and pump fresh seawater back in. The council promised funding to refurbish the pool in celebration of its thirtieth birthday in 2014, but the money never materialised.

Also keen for a swim is Sinéad Gaughan. She has arranged for a gang of swimmers to join us for our Sunday morning rite. About twenty-five people arrive despite the cool, overcast weather. It appears to be a de facto

The ladies of Belmullet take to the pool of a Sunday morning.

women's-only swimming spot, with all of the men in attendance standing on the sideline, hanging on for the cakes and hot toddies to follow.

Sinéad remembers 'walking the greasy pole' as a young girl, which sounds like a suspect euphemism but is in fact a game played at the pier 500m up the road. 'An ESB pole was covered in margarine. The game was to walk out on the pole and stand for as long as you could.' The current Water Safety Officer, Liz Healy, is also in attendance, with an enormous chocolate cake and a flask of Baileys coffee. I've prepared a hot drop too, a gallon of warm water to throw over the head à la the Myrtleville swimmers. 'It's very exotic looking,' I tell Sinead, admiring the pool. 'Did you hear that? "Very exotic," he says,' and it raises a laugh.

Through time and familiarity the pool is no longer strange or unusual to local swimmers, yet it's like no other in the country, enjoying warmer, calmer waters, fending off the pulsing sea on the other side of the wall.

BELMULLET TIDAL POOL

Latitude: 54.217389
Longitude: -9.990188

Type: Bathing, laps.

When: High to low tide.

Access: The pool is set by the Shore Road in Belmullet, off the R313.

Safety: Safe water. The tidal pool is allocated two lifeguards six days per week in July and August.

10
Sligo

36 Enniscrone

Lesson one: When you're lying down on your chest, your feet should be touching the end of the surfboard. **Lesson two**: Look over your shoulder and pick your wave. Start paddling before it arrives and keep paddling once it does. **Lesson three**: Once you're moving with the wave, pop up. Don't just lift your belly off the board. If you get up too slowly, your weight will shift to the back of the board and sink your ship.

This is my third time surfing, but my first surfing lesson. And it's badly needed. On previous occasions surfing in Cornwall and Devon I spent 95 per cent of the time paddling out beyond the breaking waves and the other 5 per cent quickly popping up to a sixty-degree angle, quickly losing balance and tumbling sideways from the board, yet I still managed to have the time of my life. I wonder how enjoyable it would be if I could actually surf.

And I don't know if it's the lesson or all the time spent in the sea this summer, or maybe it's just third time lucky, but I'm no sooner in the water

Enniscrone Beach.

than I've caught my first wave. The breaker grows in weight and strength, and the barrel looms overhead. All I can see is crashing green water in front of me and a circle of light at the end of the rolling tunnel, but I pick up speed and push through. Or that's how I remember it, at least, as I'm washed up in 15cm of tranquil water on the shoreline of this large, calm beach. I'll have to check the footage with the Red Bull camera crew in the chopper above. Or maybe Michael will set me straight.

Today, when the surf is small, it's mostly kids and parents in the water. The little lightweights can get moving on any old ripple, whereas adults need a larger force to put them in motion. While surfing can be practised as a sport, it's more obviously a form of play. The kids spend as much of the two hours mucking about as they do learning to surf. Niki Battle, one of the surf instructors, holds the board for one boy as he does a headstand. When the wave comes in, Niki gives the board a push and the boy surfs to shore upside-down.

Niki tells the kids, 'Every day you get into the sea, the water is different, the conditions are different, and every wave is doing something different. So just have respect for that. And when you're on it, just be happy and enjoy it.'

Shane Lavelle runs North West Surf School from Enniscrone Beach with the help of friends Niki and David. 'We all surf together, we all work together,' says Shane. They grew up in the area and learned to surf in Enniscrone or in nearby Easkey where the surf is bigger. 'No matter where you go in the world,' says Shane, 'every surfer knows about Easkey. My dad was a fisherman and we grew up on the water. So if I could get a loan of gear from surfers, I'd just jump in and hope for the best.'

Enniscrone, however, is perfect for learning to surf. 'It's so safe. There are no real rips on the beach. There might be rips that run over and back, but not straight out.'

You may have noticed by now that we've absconded from our duty to swimming. However, surfing – particularly if you're as bad at it as I am – involves a lot of paddling, which keeps your arms and shoulders in great shape. It's also good for the core group muscles: 'Even while lying on the board, you're training,' says Nikki. 'Your stomach muscles just increase and increase, and when you paddle on smaller boards your back is arched so you get great drive too.'

And swimmers are likely to take to surfing quickly. David tells us 'the best thing you can do to get good at surfing is to surf. The next best thing you can do is to swim.' Anything that keeps a swimmer in the sea during the winter months has to be a good thing. As the open-sea swimming season ends, the surf season kicks off with big swells heaving in up and down the west coast.

The lads don't need to venture too far from home to surf the big waves. 'A lot of the time you spend looking for offshore winds,' says Shane, 'where the wind is blowing towards the land and keeping a nice shape on the waves rolling in from the Atlantic. In Australia you'd have to travel a hundred miles or more just to find the right surf. Here you're spoiled for choice. If we're travelling to Bundoran for the day we'd consider it a big day trip. They're shpeakin' funny up there and everything.'

I wonder what the surf is like closer to home. 'If you were stuck in Dublin,' I ask, 'where would you go?'

'The pub,' says Shane.

Learning the basics with North West Surf School on Enniscrone Beach.

ENNISCRONE

Latitude: 54.213009
Longitude: -9.097672

Type: Surfing, bathing, distance swimming.

When: High to low tide.

Access: N59, then on to the R297, finally on to Bridge Street.

Safety: Sheltered beach with lifeguards. Lost its blue flag in 2015, but is generally clean and clear.

Catching wee waves.

(37) Rosses Point

'I'm not one for the wetsuits, I must say. Too much fannying about. You have to get the head wet. That's the rule really, isn't it? You haven't gone in unless you've got the head wet.'

When it comes to the quick dip, I tend to agree with Kevin. Particularly if the purpose of the swim is to get the head wet, to clear the head even, there's no point bothering with the faff of a wetsuit. During the winter months, you spend less time in the water than you do kicking and pulling the legs of the suit from your ankles.

Kevin Barry is a novelist and short story writer. He's had many addresses since his first in Limerick, but he has settled now in the former RIC barracks in Ballinafad at the foot of the Curlew Mountains. 'My most regular swim now is a five-minute cycle from the house, off a little pier, down into the lake. It's lovely and it's refreshing, but it's not the same as a sea swim. I love going on holidays and getting into the warm water, somewhere like Majorca, but the ultimate for me is the Atlantic. It's the one you grow up with, I suppose.'

Kevin has been in and out of the sea since he was a boy, but didn't get his stroke straight till the age of thirty. 'We had a municipal pool in Edinburgh,

Brendan chats with Kevin Barry (left) in the sea.

Benbulbin from Rosses Point.

and within two or three weeks I was doing lengths. Since then, it's become my main kind of exercise. I jog a bit and I do go out on the bike. But the swimming is the best craic really, you know. When you're in the water you're thinking about nothing else, you really switch off from everything. Someone said to me, going into the sea is like pressing your reset button, like you're rebooting the system.'

Michael has spotted a few compass jellyfish on our swim and Kevin's mention of Majorca brings up memories for me of the single, mysterious sting I received on my first foreign holiday there at the age of eleven. I recall the great long welts, like a burn scar, that lingered on my arm for months. 'You're completely paranoid about the jellyfish, aren't you,' says Kevin. 'It's not something I used to think of, but forever more, because of you, I will be thinking of burn scars. No one will be getting into the water after this book, I tell you.'

We swim the length of the Rosses Point Beach and back, stopping every fifty metres for a breath and a chat. 'I've been trying to perfect the butterfly,' says Kevin, 'I kind of have the arms but I can't get the legs going at all.'

Kevin and Michael drying off.

A father and daughter take a leap together off the pier.

Michael takes a late evening swim in Deadman's Point.

For Kevin, the swim, like the cycling and the running, is a way of getting out of the house, in contact with other people and staying sane. 'When you're doing readings and the like, people often ask you where do the stories come from. I used to say that because there's a lot of dialogue in the stories, it comes from the way we talk, how we abuse and misuse the English language. When I started to think about my individual stories, it struck me then that was all bollocks. Most of them come from getting out of the house, which is a very important thing for a writer to do, you know. And very often from going out on the bike or walking the cliffs around the west.'

Myself and Michael have been getting out of the house, so to speak, all summer long, watching the material appear before our very eyes. And Kevin does the same. 'The seaside, it's great for stirring up memories, childhood stuff and family stuff that you always return to. When you're in that memorious place it's going to stir up material.'

Kevin has spoken before about the reverbs and atmosphere that certain places secrete. So what about Rosses Point? 'You'd always think of Yeats, who was into taking tinctures of cannabis, which you could get then in the chemist in Sligo. He used to be down here, stoned, rolling around the beach at midnight. So you have to think of Willie when you're here.

'You could get it up until the early part of the twentieth century in chemist shops. It was used for gum diseases and the like, but if you fucked about with it, it'd get you high. I like Rosses round about early May. I love it when it's empty. I come here early in the morning. I've been meaning to do a night swim here at some point too. It's a nice handy place for a night swim actually. It's safe; you're not going to get into any difficulties.'

We leave Kevin and return later for our own evening swim, about 200 metres around the bend to Deadman's Point. As Kevin rightly says, the beach is safe, but Deadman's can be a little trickier. It's an open-ended concrete swimming pool. Why someone didn't bother to build the final wall is beyond me. A warning sign on the pathway down depicts a stick man being swept out to sea by the current. However, within the bounds of the three walls, all seems safe. An elderly man casting his line out to sea deters Michael and me from swimming any further than the pier wall.

This is the setting for my sole childhood memory of Sligo – my dad whipping on a pair of Speedos in the spitting rain as my brother, my mam and I wait in the car, looking out at a grey sky resting on grey concrete, with a sliver of grey sea cut between them. And me trying to understand the incongruity of his beaming smile and his pink-cold skin – a return for him to his childhood days in Rosses Point.

Fishing for mackerel off the end of the pier at Deadman's Point.

Sligo town decked out to celebrate Yeats' centenary year.

Rosses Point.

ROSSES POINT

Latitude: 54.306995
Longitude: -8.576666

Type: Bathing, distance swimming (from beach to Deadman's Point or vice versa).

When: High-tide only at Deadman's Point. High or low tide for the beach.

Access: Take the R219 from Sligo town. Aim for Sligo Yacht Club if swimming in Deadman's Point or take a right turn just before that for the beach.

Safety: Safe beach. Deadman's Point warns against swimming, currents at play beyond the open pool.

38 Bishop's Pool

The narrow, surly barman in the Quay Bar that overlooks Mullaghmore Pier is determined to be useless. For a start, he's giving each Guinness a solid four minutes before adding the head. He's delighted by his limited range of Bulmers – 'Draught or can?' he repeats – to the frustration of the gent alongside me trying to order a bottle for his wife. 'Draught or can?' So when I come to enquire about the origin of the name 'Bishop's Pool' from the same barman, I know full well I'm not going to get the long answer.

Me: 'I'm just wondering if you know where Bishop's Pool got its name?'

Barman: 'Bishop used to swim in it.'

Me: 'Do you know how far back that goes?'

Bishop's Pool as the tide recedes.

Michael catches the sun on his back as he swims.

Barman: 'Haven't a clue.'

Me: 'Do you know anyone around who might know?'

Barman: 'No. There's a pamphlet up at reception. That might have something on it.'

I return from the hotel reception empty-handed, but Michael has been busy on the Google machine. He discovers that Bishop's Pool is so called because it appears in the shape of a bishop's crozier. Indeed it does. It would seem to make the barman look the fool I suspected he was; however, he may still be right. It's likely enough that in the hundreds, or perhaps thousands, of years during which the pool has been filling and emptying its tidal waters that, as he so eloquently put it, 'Bishop used to swim in it.' Or that a bishop was patrolling the area, fending off licentious female bathers attempting to corrupt the morals of respectable, nude men.

Benbulben seen from the road back to Sligo.

Three teenage girls are drying off as we arrive after lunch. We've missed high tide by about three hours and the water is dropping at the rate of an inch every three minutes. But there's still enough in it for a swim, if not a dive. The water is cool and the intermittent sunshine catches the varying colours of the rock-pool floor. Miniature rock pools are revealed by the outflowing tide where little fish dart and dash as your shadow passes over.

The pool is dangerous in rough weather, with waves breaking over the rocks at high tide. Indeed surfers travel from far and wide to surf the 50-foot-high waves that break along Mullaghmore Head. On the drive to Mullaghmore the impossibly large Classiebawn Castle comes into view. It's difficult to believe that one man – inevitably a man – could possess such an estate. This was not any man's home, merely the holiday home of Lord Louis Mountbatten before his fishing boat was bombed by the Provisional IRA. The blast killed Mountbatten along with his grandson Nicholas Knatchbull, and his friend and crewmember, Paul Maxwell.

As we sit and sup our pints, I realise that the pier from which Lord Mountbatten set out lobster potting and tuna fishing in August 1979 is the very same that we overlook now, where Mountbatten's boat, *Shadow V*,

BISHOP'S POOL

Latitude: 54.472863
Longitude: -8.455594

Type: Bathing.

When: Higher tides.

Access: Drive through Mullaghmore, sticking to the coast road. The pool is located on the most northerly tip of the headland.

Safety: At full tide the water breaks over the rocks so apply common sense when deciding whether or not to swim.

was moored the night when Thomas McMahon attached the fatal time bomb.

This summer Prince Charles visited Mullaghmore for the first time since the death of his great-uncle. He spoke of the hurt the loss had caused him, and the understanding for others on this island who had lost loved ones in similarly tragic circumstances. The world was edging forward. I couldn't help but wonder if Mountbatten and those two boys had swum in Bishop's Pool, too.

Brendan cruising just below the surface.

Silver Strand

11

Donegal

(39) Rougey Rocks

We make our way from Sligo into Donegal. It's only 15km from Bishop's Pool to Bundoran but for about three of those kilometres, without our knowing it, we're driving along the Leitrim coastline, the shortest in the country. The coastline is not something Leitrim boasts about, but then again, I'm not sure if humble Leitrim boasts about anything.

Bundoran's West End must have got jealous of Kilkee's glorious Pollock Holes. Into its limestone landscape it has walled in a piece of the sea for itself, a large L-shaped pool that appears to be little-used nowadays. We are on the lookout for a sea stack to dive off, Rougey Rocks, with its fabled diving board. It seems too good to be true. Closer to town, in front of Waterworld and below the redeveloped promenade, we spot an incongruous sea stack rising up beside another man-made pool, but the pool is not deep enough for diving. In fact, it's so overfilled with sand it's not even deep enough for a swim.

But from here we can see across Bundoran's beach to another two sea stacks. When we get closer we're taken aback at how perfect this spot is for swimming. The pair of sea stacks seem to reach out over a narrow, deep-water inlet, their ledges ideal for jumps from various heights. Set between

Not the first time this has happened.

them is the coveted springboard with a drop of about 5ft that increases as the tide recedes.

As Michael points out, the diving board levels the playing field. Each swimmer is confronted with, quite literally, the same platform. It sticks its tongue out towards the sea and provokes all swimmers who step near. And so the one-upmanship begins. But it's certainly safer to have a board here than not; it offers an alternative – or temporary distraction at least – from the tall sea stacks on either side. Even for two grown men, who know full well that the water demands respect, the sea confronts us as a dangerous foe or a coaxing playmate for us (often foolishly) to pit ourselves against.

After some jumps and dives from the board, we're joined by three teenagers: Thea from Derry, and Matthew and Hannah from Dundalk. They've been holidaying in Bundoran and Rossnowlagh almost every summer of their lives. The jumps here, like those at Salthill, are a rite of passage for the young who swim in the area. Thea is the most confident swimmer of the three. She swims for her school and surfs in the sea too.

The head-first dives executed by Michael and me are outclassed by Thea's twisting backflips. She guides us up the rocks of the steeper sea stack.

First to the Ladies' Jump (a good 25ft), and then to the Men's Jump (another 5ft higher).

I feel like I'm hanging in the air for an age, and on entry I leave my mouth ever so slightly ajar. The water rushes in at such a pace that my gums bleed. Thea jumps too but leans forward; she is winded by the smack of the water against her stomach. It's another reminder, if it were needed, that the sea is as safe a place as you make it, that you are as safe as the decisions you make. But to deter people of any age from pitting themselves against themselves goes against our natural instinct and fascination for the challenges that the sea proffers.

Thea takes to the Men's Jump.

Michael, graceful as ever.

ROUGEY ROCKS

Latitude: 54.48518
Longitude: -8.281412

Type: Bathing, diving.

When: Higher tides for safer diving. Check depths either way.

Access: Car park by beach in Bundoran. Walk to the right of the beach on the Rougey Walk. Take steps towards sea stacks from promenade.

Safety: No lifeguard. As dangerous as the decisions you make.

40 Silver Strand

Silver Strand from the far side.

I t's my last time calling into Michael's on Dublin's North Great George's Street, but instead of heading down Dorset Street for the M50, we stay due north for the N3, up the Navan Road, rolling towards Cavan. Our mobile phones start roaming as we enter Enniskillen, the petrol prices change from euro to sterling, and flags of varying provenance are flying. Lumpy, black clouds threaten rain; we can guess what the skies have in store for us.

We meet Michael's old college friend, Alison Keane, just outside Donegal town. Ali is with her three kids, among whom is Molly, who is hoping to get onto the BA course in photography at IADT in Dún Laoghaire – the same college where Michael and Alison first met. Molly is joining us to make some headway on her portfolio.

From Donegal town we drive further west, through Glencolmcille and on to Malin Beg as we round corners with breathtaking views. We stop in

Michael takes an underwater selfie.

Brendan singing the *Baywatch* theme tune in his head.

View back to the many steps leading down to the beach.

the sun to take photos only to be soaked in a downpour that we should have seen coming. As we take the last corner, Silver Strand comes into view. Arms of foliage-covered cliffs sweep around the horseshoe beach, protecting it from onshore winds and creating a suntrap. The view is awe-inspiring and the 167 steps are easily taken, on the way down at least. Molly clicks away at the camera as we prepare to get in; it's terrible now to be on the receiving end of the lens. But we suck in, flex and persevere.

Michael runs the length of the beach to warm up as I toe around in the sand – soft and dark bronze – which makes for a genuinely 'snotgreen sea'. We undress and race seaward; the waves break at a heavenly rhythm with enough force to distract us from the cold. It's the kind of swim that will set your mattress swaying as you fall asleep at night. We duck-dive beneath the waves, kick legs, take sea-selfies and bask in the vivid colours of this sea.

As I trek back up the steps I remember comments I have seen on TripAdvisor. Visitors to Silver Strand tend to deduct the coveted fifth star – this remote geological feature has inconsiderately formed without a lift or escalators.

At the top of the cliff my nosiness brings me across farmland and I send sheep scattering; even a ram rears out of my way as I search for the perfect panoramic photo. I trudge eastward through waterlogged fields of darting rabbits, up to a road that looks as though it hasn't been travelled in a hundred years or more. My runners fill with cool water at every step as I slip down into a valley and back up the hill on the other side. We've been blue-sky hunting all day, and when I turn around, the scene couldn't be better or bluer.

Michael has known Molly since she was a baby. On our way back in the car, he talks music with her and her friend Josephine. I put on my Spotify playlist, our only source of distraction since the carwash swept the aerial off the roof of the Yaris. The playlist is comprised of songs amalgamated from the collection of a friend with far superior taste, plus a few of my own choosing. The massive gap in our ages becomes evident. The girls have heard of Fatboy Slim but not the Housemartins or The Beautiful South. They know vaguely who Justin Timberlake is but have never heard of 'N Sync. (I should stress that neither 'N Sync nor JT appear on the playlist.) We settle on a common appreciation of Van Morrison, and head towards Donegal town for the food festival later that evening.

Michael and Brendan in the water with their cameras.

SILVER STRAND

Latitude: 54.664663
Longitude: -8.775812

Type: Bathing, distance swimming.

When: High to low tide.

Access: R263 through Glencolmcille to Malin Beg. Car park at the end of the village.

Safety: No lifeguard. Safe, sheltered beach.

41) Ballymastocker Bay

Having spent the night outside Donegal town in the home and company of Ali, Molly and family, we drive up to Ballymastocker Strand, just south of Portsalon, in search of the cure.

I am aware that Ballymastocker was once named the second most beautiful beach in the world. However, the only evidence of this fact is on the websites of Irish and county tourism boards, keen on increasing visitor numbers in Donegal. The list had been compiled, according to one online article written in 2010, 'some years ago'. I wonder who exactly ranks these beaches.

What makes for a good beach, in any person's opinion, will probably change from day to day, depending on their shifting desires and circumstances. Michael and I are continually asked what our favourite places to swim are. The answer is invariably 'the last place we swam at', having heightened recollections of the previous day's dip. But a more considered answer would depend on whether you're looking for a quick plunge or a distance swim, a

Behind the beach at Ballymastocker.

high dive or a sea lounge, whether you've brought a picnic and a good book, or if you're just looking to get cold, wet and refreshed on your commute to work. What I can say about Ballymastocker Strand is that it is an exceedingly fine beach. And on a sunny day, like many another beach along Ireland's coastline, it's deserving of at least a Top Ten spot.

Particularly stunning is the eastern end, set against high, rocky dunes that finger out as far as the shoreline. But it is a swimmers' beach as well as a beauty spot: a full 2km in length, and a swim to the pier at Portsalon will extend that by another half a kilometre.

The tide is out on our arrival, leaving acres of soft white sand before us. We are meeting Patrick Corkery, one of the original book's Kickstarter backers and Twitter followers. My main concern has been to get here in time and find him. It isn't until we arrive and meet up that I start to wonder about what kind of a swim Patrick is expecting. His Twitter profile is @PTKswims, with the tagline: 'Wants to be in the water all the time.' I should have paid more attention to these signs. Indeed, he has made a four-hour drive for a day's swimming and will drive the same distance back tomorrow. Now, as we step over the dunes together, with a stunning low-tide, white-sand beach coming into view, I explain that Michael and I aren't the best men for long distances, that I'll stay in for maybe fifteen or twenty minutes, Michael a little longer perhaps.

After a quick photo shoot, we swim the eastern extent of the beach. Patrick soon realises we're not going to keep up, but he also works out that we won't drown either, so he swims on ahead. When I catch up, he is on his way back wearing a wig of kelp, fixed to his head with his goggle straps – a proper Rasta swimmer.

After about 400m of front crawl and breaststroke (I am still reverting to the breaststroke), I decide to exit and get dry. I feel the post-swim endorphin rush. And for the first time on our two-month journey, I lie down on my towel and bask in the sun. In a summerful of beaches, it occurs to me as odd that I've not taken the time to sunbathe till now. Michael and I usually spend

BALLYMASTOCKER BAY

Latitude: 55.188208
Longitude: -7.609341

Type: Bathing, distance swimming.

When: High to low tide.

Access: Car park by beach in Bundoran town. Walk right of the beach on the Rougey Walk. Take steps towards sea stacks from promenade.

Safety: Safe blue-flag beach with lifeguard.

up to three or four hours at a location. But when not sampling the quality of the swim, we're out walking dunes, checking depths, reading information and warning signs, taking photos, waiting on tides, or squeezing passers-by for any stories or gossip.

It is the penultimate day of our summer's journey and as I lie on the towel I think back – my memories already tinged with nostalgia – to the places we've visited, the friends we've made, and the beaches and pools where we've swum. How do I say this without sounding ridiculous? I feel the deepest sense of contentment possible and hold back tears.

The winding road up the hillside offers fantastic views over the beach.

42 Harry's Hole

On leaving Portsalon, our party grows from three to five as we pick up my old friend Stephen Mangan, who I've known since Junior Infants, and our new friend David Lopez, a Colombian living and working in Dublin.

We travel in convoy to Marblehill Beach, and then on a couple of hundred metres to the little cove at its northern end. Scores of holiday homes are clustered around this little beach, the centre of activity around which holiday routines are made and played out. It's early evening; the last swimmers lounge in the high tide, kids come in for dinner and adults make their way back to the seafront with bottles of wine in hand. The air fills with barbeque smoke and the smell of searing meat.

From here we set out on foot over the headland to Harry's Hole, our bare legs scraping through juniper needles. We look down to see tropical blue waters lit by the evening sun as it shifts its light past thick clouds. A French couple in wetsuits dive from a rock of their own. A mother watches her three blonde girls showing off for the camera. I soon learn that she is a triathlete from Derry who trains with the triathlon club at Ned's Point on the Inishowen Peninsula. The two men with her are also triathletes, one of whom has recently completed the half-Ironman in Dublin. They recommend a number of other beaches on the Inishowen Peninsula, but the summer is drawing to a close and we simply don't have the time to visit them: Kinnego, Culdaff, Five Fingers Beach. These are all remarkably beautiful spots and easy to find. Harry's Hole is another example of a swimming spot you won't have heard of unless you know the area well. I got the tip-off from Maurice Earls, owner of Books Upstairs on Dublin's D'Olier Street.

Like my own family, who have favoured Ballinskelligs all our lives, the Earls family are return visitors to this part of Donegal. The tendency to stick to familiar places makes sense, and the result is an intimate knowledge of perhaps only a handful of swimming spots. Donegal, for me, was a complete mystery. Many people we met in Connemara had never been to Waterford or Wexford and we talked to others from Cork and Kerry who had never swum in the Forty Foot or at Howth Head. If nothing else, our journey will hopefully connect some of the dots for swimmers and holidaymakers alike, and gently encourage people out of their comfort zones.

There's lots to explore at high and low tide here at Harry's Hole. During the spring tide, there are dives of 1m which are still jumpable at lower tides. There are some cave-lets to explore and a higher dive from a lump of rock set closer to the cliffs.

David is reluctant to swim. 'I'm used to tropical waters,' he says in his easy-listening accent which emphasises every syllable. Instead he takes out his Dublin-colours kite and flies it overhead. As the day rolls on, we learn more of Patrick Corkery's feats in the sea. He once hopped on a plane in the middle of a two-week family holiday in Spain to attempt the North Channel

Fantastic deep rock-pool experience at Harry's Hole.

The three Derry girls having fun in the water.

crossing when a cancellation gave him a two-day opening (he was taken from the water a mile from the Scottish shoreline after being stung by a multitude of Lion's Mane jellyfish). He's completed two Ice Mile swims in Lough Dan in County Wicklow, the Lake Zurich Swim (26.4km) and the Manhattan Island Marathon Swim (28.5 miles), among others.

I'm blown away by the technicalities involved in the Manhattan Island swim in particular: the start date and time each year is dictated by the tide so that the incoming tide assists them up the East River. Each swimmer is accompanied by a motorboat and a kayaker, which help them navigate twenty-odd bridges as well as the ebb and flow of three New York rivers.

The application for entry to the race is a marathon in itself. The organiser requires you to name your crew nine months in advance; they want to see evidence of articles you've written about swims (or articles that have been written about you); they want a list of distance swims you've already completed, including details on water temperature during the race, number of entrants and where you placed among them. They need to see certificates, photos, X-rays and ECGs, all in order to prove your fanaticism, conviction and ability to complete the 28.5-mile distance. Once that's cleared, you just have to hand over about €2,000 in order to compete.

A French couple mid-flight.

HARRY'S HOLE

Latitude: 55.18339
Longitude: -7.896793

Type: Bathing, diving.

When: Higher tides for safer diving.
Check depths.

Access: Turn off the N56 for Marblehill
Holiday Park. From there, walk along
the coastal trail for about 300m.

Safety: Sheltered. No lifeguard.
Take care on slippery rocks.

When strangers pass you on a crisp winter day and spot you undressing for a two-minute dip, they think – and frequently tell you – that you're mad, though it's often followed by 'Fair play to you.' So take a moment to tip your hat to the increasing number of Irish distance swimmers who, like Patrick and the other swimmers we met in Wexford, Waterford, Cork and Kerry, battle the cold waters for hours upon hours, through strong currents and gelatinised sea beasties to obtain glories that few of us will ever hear of.

(43) Fort Dunree

A 7.30 a.m. swim follows another late night. Our convoy wheels on from Buncrana towards our final swim of the summer. The Inishowen Peninsula has a coastline nearly twice the length of Dublin's but, despite all of the stunning beaches to choose from, we select a spot less known for its swimming heritage and more for its military history.

We were invited by Terry Tedstone to take a look at the small, dilapidated pier set beneath Fort Dunree, an eighteenth-century coastal defence fortification. Terry, who works in the fort, now a military museum, takes a dip there during the summer months, and small groups of teens and local artists sometimes make their way down the narrow green path for a swim in the sun. Fort Dunree has recently secured government money to restore the pier, and is now hoping to attract swimmers as well as tourists to the area.

It's not until we dive into the water that we realise what an incredible location this is. At high tide, the pier is plenty deep for diving. A lump of rock juts up from the water not ten yards from the pier. The sea floor beneath it is out of sight, so we climb to its highest point to plunge in. On the opposite side of the narrow pier is the fort itself, set high on a large rocky promontory with drawbridge entry. The swim from pier to fort is ideal for snorkelling

View of the narrow pier pre-renovation, from the drawbridge (left), and looking back up to the fort (right).

and at higher tides the narrow gully between the mainland and the fort is passable. Hanging over the cliff edge is a latrine whose open pipe still points down into the gully, and from which the turds of British and Irish soldiers had plummeted for over a century. It is also the site where a drunken soldier once fell to his death. On return to the fort after a night's boozing, he attempted to jump the divide where the drawbridge had been pulled up.

Through the gully and under the drawbridge we swim, but turn back before hitting the open sea. Patrick is keen on circling the fort, however. On judging the pull of the current, he thinks it wiser to swim clockwise, to take advantage of the pull from the outgoing tide. He eyes up the potential of the setting for a sea sprint race – roughly 300m from the pier, around the fort and tussling through the narrow gap to finish. A swim 1km further north along the cliff face will bring you to the beautiful, sheltered Dunree Bay.

Dunree overlooks Lough Swilly, a deep glacial fjord, from where the Earls of Tyrone and Tyrconnell fled in 1607. At the mouth of the Swilly, a French

Synchronised dip.

fleet carrying Wolfe Tone was intercepted by the British and defeated in battle in 1798. Within a decade, it was fortified by the British as a defence against Napoleonic invasion. During the First World War it became the largest staging point for the Royal Navy's Grand Fleet and was one of three naval bases that remained under British sovereignty after the Anglo-Irish Treaty – the last place in the Republic to fly a British flag on being ceded to the Free State in 1938.

We are joined this morning by artist Sinead Walsh, who practises in Artlink Studios on the grounds of the fort. She has also invited a family friend, Eberhard Rapp, who is touring Ireland to gather material for his next book of photography. He acts as our photographer for the morning and joins us in the café, which Terry opened especially for us before giving us a tour of the Fort.

Sea bathing often triggers notions of a bygone age, of Victorian splendour rusting away. The broken diving boards and cracking concrete one sometimes encounters might encourage those notions. But so many of the forty-three spots we've visited show signs of redevelopment and revitalisation

View through the narrow gully.

Dunree Beach on the northern side of the fort.

similar to Fort Dunree. Many county councils are realising the potential of their natural amenities, and under the guardianship of swimming clubs, voluntary associations and bathing enthusiasts, both locally and nationally, swimming as a hobby and a sport is clearly on the rise. Open sea swimming is a recession-proof pastime that has been helped by the rise in popularity of triathlons, bringing more people to the sea. Sea bathing is alive and legs kicking. And the sea temperature? Arrah, sure look, come on in, it's gorgeous!

FORT DUNREE

Latitude: 55.195868
Longitude: -7.55306

Type: Bathing, snorkelling, distance swimming.

When: Higher tides for full experience.

Access: Head north from Buncrana on the R238. Turn left for Glebe and continue to Dunree.

Safety: No lifeguard. Narrow walk down to pier. Check for depths before diving and beware of large rocks below surface.

Published in 2016 by
The Collins Press
West Link Park
Doughcloyne
Wilton
Cork
T12 N5EF
Ireland

First published by Six + West 2015

A CIP record for this book is available from the British Library.

Paperback ISBN: 978-1-84889-280-4
PDF eBook ISBN: 978-1-84889-584-3
EPUB eBook ISBN: 978-1-84889-585-0
Kindle ISBN: 978-1-84889-586-7

Design and typesetting by Burns Design
Typeset in New Century Schoolbook and Helvetica
Printed in Poland by Białostockie Zakłady Graficzne SA

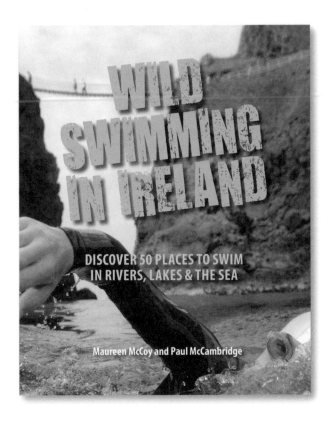

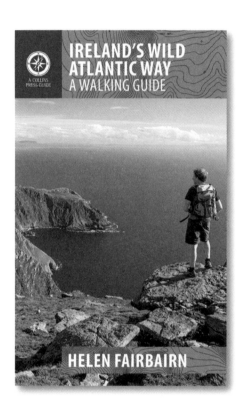
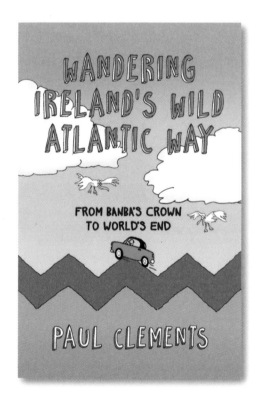